Over the Hills and Far Away

About the author

Janet Rogers worked as a news reporter in her twenties and returned to writing when she retired. She has won several national travel writing competitions and her articles have appeared in the UK and Australian press and in Bradt travel books.

She is a keen cyclist and swimmer and did her first triathlon aged 70. She lives by the sea in West Sussex.

About the illustrator

James Perry studied illustration at Northbrook College, Worthing, obtaining a BA in 2019. He enjoys bringing people's ideas to life and the creative challenge it involves. Aside from art, his interests are video games, food and exploring different cultures.

Over the Hills and Far Away

Tiny Travel Tales from Around the World

Janet Rogers

Illustrations and cover design by James Perry

Copyright

Janet Rogers 2024

Janet Rogers has asserted her right under the Copyright, Designs and Patents Act 1988 to be identified as the author of this work. All rights reserved. No part of this publication may be reproduced, stored in a retrieval system or transmitted in any form, or by any means (electronic, mechanical, or otherwise) without the prior written permission of both the copyright owners and the publisher.

Illustration copyright James Perry

Disclaimer

The contents of this book are the sole expression of the author's thoughts and opinions and do not necessarily reflect those of Amazon Kindle Direct Publishing or any other parties associated with the publication of this book. The author and publisher make no representation or warranties about the accuracy or completeness of the information contained in this book. The author and publisher assume no liability for any loss or damage caused by the use of the information contained in this book and they are not responsible for any actions taken as a result of reading this book.

ISBN

Contents

Over the Hills and Far Away..1

Preface 9

UK...1

Life of Riley 2

The Northern Lights 5

Tale of Two Statues...8

Too Much Pride 11

The Sleeping Bridesmaid................................14

Littlehampton or the Caribbean 17

The Khyber Pass 20

Ghosts and Gales on the West Highland Way 23

Kingley Vale...26

The Bluebell Line...29

The Mappa Mundi 32

Houghton Mill..35

Another Wedding 38

Skiing or Cycling? 41

Australian Adventures 44

Bondi..45

Was it a Pie Shop or a Pizza Shop?.....................48

Crocodiles..51

A Precious Find Under the Water 54

Batmen at the Opera 57

The Cassowary 60

France by Bike 63

Cycling to Paris 64

American Beaches in Normandy 67

D- Day Landing Beaches in the 21st Century 70

He Had No Soles 73

Marseille to Barcelona 76

Edge of the Land 79

Wildlife 82

Monet's Garden 85

France – 88

Apples, Artists and Wine 88

Apple Picking in Normandy 89

Christian Meeting 92

On the Bridge at Avignon 95

Bertie and the Maze 98

In the Footsteps of Van Gogh 101

Van Gogh's Final Days 105

Monsieur Bob's Search for his Vines 108

Wine Tasting 111

Treading the Grapes.................................114

Wedding Champagne.................................117

Italy.................................120

Cows and Dumplings.................................121

The Hidden Valley.................................124

The Missing Restaurant.................................127

The Long March.................................131

Sunrise in the Dolomites.................................134

A Cake Decorator's Dream.................................137

A Big Muddy Hole.................................140

Path of the Gods.................................143

Sri Lanka.................................146

Elephant Procession.................................147

Hindu Blessing.................................150

The Waiting Game.................................153

Looking for Leopards.................................156

Incident at Lion Rock.................................159

Malaysia, Thailand, Cambodia and Vietnam..........162

A Breath of Sea Air.................................163

The Border Crossing.................................166

Sharm's Story.................................169

The Fall and Rise of a Cyclist.................................171

Odds and Ends..174

Mozart and Maria..175

Waking the Dead 178

Nootka Island..181

The Wonky City 184

Greek Island Heaven or Hell...............................187

The Shoes 189

Preface

My first travel adventure was as an 18-year-old, hitch hiking through Europe. Unfortunately, or maybe fortunately I didn't write it down.

I worked as a journalist in my twenties and the writing foundations were laid then. A long gap followed and I only really got back to writing when I retired. Since then, I've concentrated mainly on travel writing.

As far as travel is concerned, photographs aren't quite enough. I want to write down the experience because I find that nothing cements it in my mind as strongly as the written word. Show me a photograph of where I've travelled and I can see that place. Show me a piece of writing and I'm back in the very moment, experiencing the sights, sounds and smells.

You'll notice that there are quite a few cycling tales. I've done a number of long-distance cycling tours because I find that they are the best way to see and get to know places. The key elements are that the pace is slow and the experience is right up close. You can't miss anything or anyone and there's always time to stop and chat and take an even closer look, if only to examine the elephant's muddy footprints on the tarmac!

I started writing 500-word pieces for a Telegraph weekly travel competition. After I'd won the competition half a dozen times, I found I could distil certain travel experiences quickly and efficiently into 500 words. I could capture the moment, work out a beginning, a middle and an end and produce a complete mini tale.

I did this regularly and found I had such a collection of tales that I decided to put them together in a book. They're great for people who can't face long complicated travel pieces with detailed descriptions. They are literally snippets or postcards from my travels. I hope you enjoy them.

UK

I'm starting with the UK and moving on to more exotic locations later in the book. I wanted to show that you don't have to go far to find interesting people and places. My home village is close to Littlehampton in West Sussex so for the piece entitled 'Littlehampton or the Caribbean' I made my shortest journey - two miles.

The Life of Riley which is set in the Yorkshire Dales, was a runner up in the Guardian travel writing competition and the judge commented that it was 'a wonderful thumbnail sketch which was evocative and well observed and came with a clever and witty final note.' His words, not mine but I'm happy with that!

The Tale of Two Statues comes from my frequent visits to Twickenham and discovering the other statue hidden in the undergrowth down by the river. Most visitors to the Twickenham Stadium will never have seen the nymphs at play in the riverside gardens.

I have included two personal wedding pieces, not exactly travel tales but I hope they give a sense of the place as well as the occasion.

Life of Riley

George sat in the corner of the bar sucking air through the gaps where his teeth used to be. He was consuming large quantities of beer and whisky, named after moorland sheep and birds.

"Them's millionaires," he said, nodding in the direction of a group of young men, flush with four legged friends and four-wheel drives. I'd seen them that morning, vehicles parked on the cobbled forecourt of the old inn, high in the Yorkshire Dales; men wearing flat caps and body warmers and woolly socks with tasselled bits at the top, strutting around with guns over their shoulders.

A man entered the bar with a dog on a lead. A cacophony of barking broke out. Dogs emerged from under tables and dark corners. Sleeping dogs stirred and joined in the fray. The barking subsided and the dogs settled back, camouflaged on the grey flagstones. This was doggy heaven, I thought; wild moors to roam all day, grouse and rabbits to chase and, at night, lounging in front of log fires. It was human heaven too.

We had travelled from the south to places with foreign sounding names like Yockenthwaite and Hubberholme and strange words such as grikes and ginnels. We thought we were staying in Pateley Bridge but when we arrived and asked for the Crown Inn, the traffic warden shook his head and stared with the vacant gaze of a sheep.

I looked again at our instructions and in small print, just before the name, Pateley Bridge, was the word Middlesmoor. That was the clue. We snaked round single-track roads, hemmed in by dry stone walls and climbed to the top of the moors. We were almost 1000 feet up in a tiny village where the stone houses seemed to cling to a network of steep paths. From our bedroom window in the old inn, we could look down on valley pastures.

Later that afternoon we ambled in the dale; it was warm and balmy and the sky was speckled with white cloud. We passed through meadows of creamy thistledown floating in the breeze. We skirted a pine forest and returned through a field of black cows.

The next day we awoke to a thick mist, the trees and buildings just shadows and beyond them, nothing. The hills, once emerald and lime green, had disappeared under a white sheet. We walked in rain among the remains of ancient settlements, parts of walls and piles of stones, everything lying in a mess, no order, just flung down and embedded in the landscape, and claimed by the sheep who wandered through it.

We returned to our hill top inn for dinner. George was still in the corner, supping beer and whisky. The shooting party were celebrating. The dogs were resting. A retriever came up and nudged me. I stroked him and asked his name. "That there's Riley," the publican said.

"This is the life, isn't it," I said as I patted him. And I'm sure Riley nodded.

The Northern Lights

He promised me a trip to see the Northern Lights. But it hasn't turned out quite as I expected.

I walk outside as darkness falls and I do see great swathes of blue and green light swirling above. And there are rows of purple and pink and yellow lights and a giant flashing wand pointing heavenwards, like a rocket about to launch.

But I am unmoved. Blackpool, the country's great illuminator and master of illusion, has yet to harness the natural phenomenon that is the aurora borealis.

I walk along the seafront and stare up at the weird and gaudy plastic blobs, flashing and shining in a lighting frenzy. A tram disguised as a boat, floats by and then another disguised as a plane. A million bulbs and six miles of lights, brush over the town's imperfections and bring colour and sparkle to its fading façade. A hundred fish and chip bars beckon, taunting my nostrils with the aroma of fat.

Blackpool Illuminations, billed as the greatest free lightshow on earth, have been a major part of the town's tourist trade since 1879 when they were described as "artificial sunshine."

In daylight I'd seen the litter swirling in the gutter, the peeling paint, the rusty metal seats and grey wires hanging like spaghetti above the seafront road. I'd ambled on the pier, past dodgems and a darts stall with a giant stuffed turtle flopped over the counter.

At the end of the pier, I had read the memorials to two young men. Red carnations and red roses were attached to the railings. A lifebelt had been left loose from its casing, the rope uncoiled ready for use.

Darkness has come now and wiped away the blemishes but I sense that the bright lights conceal more than peeling paint. I return to my hotel to lie in a darkened room and give my eyes some relief from the flashing lights.

I awake early. The smell of cooked breakfasts is wafting through my window. I want to walk on a deserted beach, dip my toes in the sea and breathe in the fresh sea air.

The sun is rising behind the seafront hotels as I walk down the elegant sandstone steps which swirl in a graceful curve from one pier to the next. The tide is out and a seagull is peering at its reflection in a silver pool. At the water's edge, the wind catches the top of the breaking wave and blows up a pure white wisp of spray. The sun is lighting up the sand now and turning it golden.

A group of children are running in and out of the waves, laughing. A horse box is unloading donkeys. There are still simple pleasures to be enjoyed among the dazzle. I turn and look back at the seafront. The colours are muted from this distance, a mere silhouette lit up by the rising sun. This is Blackpool's best illumination, I decide. I'll have to travel a lot further north to get anything better.

Tale of Two Statues

I stand surrounded by the legs of giants and stare up at the blue sky. I am a Lilliputian in a strange land. Five burly men lifting, reaching and jumping in graceful poses and at the very top an oval ball balanced on the tips of fingers.

This is Twickenham's newest statue and one now familiar to those who frequent the home of England rugby. It has pride of place on the piazza in front of the stadium's south stand. The 27 ft bronze sculpture depicts a rugby line-out. It was erected at a cost of more than £400,000.

Engraved around the bottom of the statue are the core values that tell people what rugby is all about – teamwork, respect, enjoyment, discipline and sportsmanship.

But, at the other end of the town there is another statue, much older and little known in rugby circles, of naked nymphs and winged horses. It is hidden away in greenery down by the river.

Twickenham is a town of two faces. On match days it puts on its rugby mask. The town hums with activity and good humour. Purposeful people, busy like ants, search out friends, weave through tangled crowds and bump into old mates. There is much chatting, drinking and laughing.

Little stalls, set up in the gardens of houses, sell doughnuts, and sausages and burgers as local residents feed the hungry visitors. A hint of fried onions wafts in the air. A blue haze settles over the area like the medina in Marrakesh. There are no snake charmers but England supporters always hope for a little magic on the field.

Stalls sell scarves, hats and flags, the colours changing as quickly as the opposition. And always in your ear, the urgent whisper of the ticket tout. "Have you got any extras, any spares."

I go in search of the other statue. I walk through the town, past pubs with posses of beer drinkers standing outside enjoying the winter sun, supping their first pint with the taste of breakfast still fresh on the palate.

I reach the river and watch the ducks splashing, geese landing and swans preening and, on the opposite shore, the oarsmen launching their boats and rowing down the river. I walk a little further along the river path and catch a glimpse of white marble shapes in the shrubbery. There it is. The other statue, a cluster of naked nymphs adorning a cascade and pool in the riverside gardens of York House.

Some are sitting on rocks or scallop shells, some are climbing. All are reaching and stretching and gazing up at Venus standing naked on the backs of two prancing, winged horses. The central nymph is holding up, not a rugby ball, but a pearl.

The game is over now. But the bronze giants are still wrestling for the ball. Red rose petals are squashed under foot. Leaves rustle in the gutters. The blue haze lifts and life in this attractive riverside town returns to normal. Down by the river the nymphs are still playing in the pools and searching for pearls.

Too Much Pride

It was the squat, white sign by the side of the road that gave it away. It contained two letters painted in black, WR.

"This used to be Yorkshire. It might still be Yorkshire," we said. "WR stands for West Riding." We uttered the words with a certain triumph, a feeling of mild euphoria, even though the rain dripped from our noses and our socks seemed to have drowned in our boots.

Our Lancastrian friend, Bob, looked defiant. "It's definitely not Yorkshire," he declared. How could this wonderful area which he had known all his life, where he'd explored and trekked and wandered as a student, be part of that other county. He tried to think of an explanation. "WR. It's probably something to do with the water authority," he said.

We smirked and remained silent. Bob had enticed us to his land with a promise of three days' walking in beautiful Lancashire. "You'll love it. It's a wonderful county," he said, his chest swelling with pride. And he proceeded to proclaim its beauty at every twist in the road, every majestic fell and every bubbling brook.

And the brooks were certainly bubbling. Lancashire was awash. It was as though a tidal wave was sweeping over the land.

Cascades of water raced and tumbled, spewing through gaps in dry stone walls, swamping fields, pouring through gateways and leaving sludgy trails of debris. Only the sheep chewed on, seemingly unaware of the clatter around them.

But the rain didn't bother us. We were swept along by the wind and Bob's enthusiasm. We left the cocoon of our country inn, the log fires, rugs on flagstones, comfy sofas and plump cushions, and ventured out. We brave, soft southerners with our hardy, northern friend. We were walking in the little known and sparsely populated Forest of Bowland, 300 square miles of wild moorland and fell.

It's great isn't it," Bob enthused. And we had to agree; it was beautiful, even in the rain. But there's such a thing as pride overload. And we'd reached the point where we just wanted to gag him, to wipe away the self-satisfied grin. The sign by the side of the road was a gift.

Later over a drink in the bar at the old inn, someone produced electronic evidence that the area had indeed been part of Yorkshire, right up to the time when Bob was a student and enjoying all it had to offer. And then in the reorganisation of local government in the 70s, Yorkshire relinquished it and it became part of Lancashire.

"They didn't want it. Largely uninhabited and little known, it's not surprising, is it?" we teased.

For a moment Bob looked downcast. "I can't believe it." he said. Then he declared defiantly: "Anyway it's great. You should see it on a good day."

The Sleeping Bridesmaid

The flowers are dry like tissue paper now. The pink roses have faded but the garland hangs on my bedroom mirror as a reminder of that special day. The day the tiny bridesmaid wrenched the ring of flowers from her head and flung it on the ground and collapsed exhausted on the church pew and slept; her gold dress draping over her thin ankles, her golden hair lying like skeins of silk on polished wood.

She lay in a deep and peaceful sleep, undisturbed by vows and promises and by readings about love and singing about feet walking in ancient times on England's green mountains.

She missed the seriousness and sensitivity of the bespectacled priest who seemed unable to smile even as he told how he had prayed for a fine day for the wedding. His concern was that if all priests prayed for good weather for their wedding couples, great swathes of rain would build up and fall in the places in between.

"Does anyone know any reason why these two people should not be joined together in holy matrimony?" He asked. He waited and sighed. Silence. "I'm always pleased to get past this point," he said.

Then there were vows, promises to love, comfort and protect, and rings to exchange. And finally the proclamation by the priest. "Those whom God has joined together, let no one put asunder."

It was all over. The register was signed, the flower girl woke and rubbed her eyes. The organ played and the bells rang out and the procession made its way down the aisle, through the porch filled with candles and out into the bright sunshine.

A clutch of tourists had formed at the bottom of the cobbled drive to the old church. "She must be famous, an actress from Emmerdale, I think," someone in the crowd whispered. The priest slipped quietly away his head bobbing above the crowds in the street. Another day's work over.

Then, all returned to the country hotel with its sloping lawns and pond of lilies and gravel paths edged with lavender and old flagstones worn and trodden, and sipped champagne to the melodic sound of tropical music and feasted on roast lamb and meringue cake with red and purple berries.

The next day, when it was all over, I walked back towards the church, over the pack horse bridge, past the weir, clear water flowing as it has done for centuries.

I climbed the hill and ambled down into the meadows along by the River Avon, catching a glimpse of the church spire across the water.

The priest's weather prayers now exhausted, a fine drizzle fell and a smell of damp nettles settled in the air. The hedgerows were plump with sloes and blackberries.

I walked back along the road, past the abbey. I stopped and picked an oak leaf and acorn from a tree.

I thought I'd give them to the happy couple because you know what they say about little acorns.

Littlehampton or the Caribbean

The elderly man turned to his wife as they stood looking out across the river. He waved his hand expansively taking in the whole scene, the far bank with its boat yards and marina, sailing boats moored in the foreground and swans flying overhead.

"And you want to go to the Caribbean?" he said indignantly. The woman pulled up the collar of her jacket against the strong south westerly and shrugged. "Well, yes."

They were standing on the east bank of the River Arun and the town, which is apparently so much better than anything in the Caribbean, is Littlehampton in West Sussex. Everyone, it seems, has a childhood memory of Littlehampton where they rode the big dipper, crashed and smashed on the bumper cars and built sandcastles on the beach.

And they will still have the smell of candy floss stored in their memory bank. Old Nora who ran the ice cream shop down by the river is no longer there but the fish and chip shops are, and the smell of chips and vinegar still lingers in Pier Road.

Today the town is different in many ways. The waterfront regeneration has transformed the area with upmarket riverside flats and houses and an attractive pedestrian walkway, an award-winning cafe design and the longest bench in the world.

But for me the best time to see the town is out of season. Choose a warm autumn day when the beaches are empty and the sea flat like glass or a winter's day when a sprinkle of frost decorates the seaweed and stones. Or a blustery day when the south westerly blows your hat off and the sky and sea merge in a palate of dull greys and the waves leap six feet high and race forward like giant white boulders in an avalanche. Or springtime when the wild sea kale grows in clumps on the pebbles, waxy leaves thick and fleshy.

At the height of summer there are still sand castles to build, and Punch and Judy shows to watch. And pedalos on the old oyster pond where the fishermen used to store their fish.

I wandered along by the river and tried to see the town with new eyes, Caribbean eyes. The swans were settling on the concrete slipway by the lifeboat station and twisting their necks under soft white wings.

The winter sun was setting over the west bank and the sky turning orange and the only sounds were the creaking boats moored at the water's edge and a metallic tinkling of halliards on masts. I returned to the seafront.

I passed a fish and chip shop. At a table near the window, I noticed the elderly man and his wife. He'd taken her out for dinner; their plates were piled high with golden battered food, spattered with tomato sauce and there was tea to wash it all down. No, it was certainly not the Caribbean. No wonder she yearned for something different.

The Khyber Pass

We are cycling towards the Khyber Pass. Not the real one in Pakistan with its history of violence and where it is said that every stone has been soaked in blood.

Our route is over the South Downs, in southern England, a track so named by local cyclists because of its steep and rough terrain. In winter it is bleak and the chalk is slippery like glass. In summer there are flints and stones to catch you unawares. In cycling circles, it is talked about softly and always with a glimmer of uncertainty in the eye.

We leave the main road and cycle along a lane shaded by oak and beech, a sweet, damp, woody smell in the air from the overnight rain. We pass flint cottages, pink and yellow dahlias behind stone walls, and, just before Burpham, we turn off and start the steep climb over the Downs.

Today the sun is shining. Pure white clouds amble across the sky nudged by a soft breeze. Hedgerows are woven with wild clematis. We pedal hard, already in our lowest gear. My chest is heaving.

My bike is also feeling the strain. It seems to be protesting at the climb, making loud metallic creaking noises. It's as though it's angry and is uttering expletives. I am not really concerned but I am getting strange looks from my fellow cyclists.

After a long, hard climb we reach the top and I clear the fog of exertion from my sunglasses. We dismount and enjoy a moment of peace, peering into the distance, down into the valley where the River Arun curls towards a distant strip of pale blue sea.

Then we take off, freewheeling down the track, the landscape unfolding like a patterned carpet, with patches of emerald and honey and bands of bottle green. My bike rattles and grunts, its vocal tics blurting out in the calm morning air.

At Houghton Bridge we stop at the riverside café for coffee and rock cakes. A fellow cyclist shakes my bike in an effort to locate its anguish and ease his own. He looks perplexed.

We travel on through small villages moulded in the lee of the swooping hills. We lunch in Duncton on thick bread with prawns and soft cheese, and drink cold beer.

Some 30 miles later my companions can contain themselves no longer. They stare intently at my bicycle, ears pricked ready to identify the offending part.

"It's the saddle," one exclaims.

"I can't bear any rattling sound," says another. "I always have to investigate."

I shrug. We stop on a grassy bank and I hand over my bike. Spanners and Allen keys appear. Nuts and bolts are tightened and loosened. Parts are prodded and pushed. The saddle is removed and replaced and removed again. Copious quantities of oil are squirted.

I mount my bike and we start the climb homewards, back over the Khyber Pass. It is as though their work has been in vain. The creaking continues. I hang back sensing their fury. We reach the top and stop by a field of sheep. They do not seem to be disturbed by the grunting of my bike.

I start the downward trek and then quite suddenly I hear only - the sound of silence. I sigh with relief and the realisation that there will be no spilling of blood on the Khyber Pass today.

Ghosts and Gales on the West Highland Way

I have just walked Scotland's most famous long-distance route, the West Highland Way, 95 miles of old military roads, drovers' tracks and footpaths.

I might have managed it more easily if I'd been a tadpole. I would have had to wiggle my tail furiously to get up the slopes but my goodness I'd have hurtled down with ease.

Scotland's annual rainfall is 80 inches and I could be forgiven for thinking that most of it fell during the week of my walk. The pathways turned to rivulets, every mossy bank and stone dripped, the streams and waterfalls gurgled and gushed. The wind roared and black clouds hung ominously over the mountains. It was magnificent.

Mentally it was refreshing but physically it was more a feat of endurance. And it was the feet that did the endurance. The conversation every evening as the walkers fell into their bed and breakfast accommodation was not about the wildlife and flaming gorse but about strained knees and swollen ankles. Walkers swapped elastic knee bandages and tubes of arnica with the furtiveness of drug dealers.

You can walk the West Highland Way in as many days as you like but to a large extent you are governed by the accommodation available. Most people take six, seven or eight days to cover the 95 miles from Milngavie, just north of Glasgow, to Fort William.

The West Highland Way provides a feast of stunning and varied scenery. Two days are spent skirting the east bank of Loch Lomond where oak and beech trees lean precariously over the water. Feral goats tread daintily on the steep slopes and munch their way through lush vegetation. North of the loch, the way moves into the Highlands and there are long stretches through heather moorland with fine mountain views.

One evening after we'd walked nearly 19 miles and crossed the inhospitable and bleak Rannoch Moor, we dropped down to the Kingshouse Hotel, an inn since 1800 with a long history associated with salt smuggling and cattle-droving. And ghosts.

As we lay in bed that night the wind roared across the desolate landscape. Every window and door creaked. At 5am we were awoken by a loud banging and the desperate cries of a man. "Help me! Help me!"

We listened and waited. The hotel was silent. Again, the cry came. "Help me," accompanied by a loud banging on the front door, which was just below our bedroom. No one stirred. My husband leapt from his bed and dashed downstairs. The shouting stopped. He returned minutes later and got back into bed.

"Is he alright?" I enquired.

"I don't know. There was no one there," he said. And the next morning at breakfast, no one but us, had heard desperate cries in the night.

Kingley Vale

Tread lightly among the ancient yew trees of Kingley Vale or you may disturb the ghosts of centuries. The trees have stood for more than 500 years. Some may have been around in Roman times.

Silence and mystery pervade this hidden valley in the South Downs, near Chichester, West Sussex, where these ancient trees have watched and waited for hundreds of years, their vast tentacles lolling unnervingly. To step there alone in daylight is eerie. To walk at twilight is not for the fainthearted.

Some 30 ancient trees grow at the bottom of the valley. During the past century, sheep grazing has ceased on the valley slopes and this has allowed the yew trees to spread up the sides of the valley and on to the top of the hill, resulting in one of the finest yew forests in Western Europe.

The poet Tennyson was a regular visitor to the forest and it is said that his ghost roams there still.

No one knows the exact age of the trees because the middle of all the old trees has rotted away and there are no growth rings to count. The trees have survived because, although they have no centre, the outer trunk is still alive. This has allowed the trunk to flex and bend in stormy weather. Where some of the huge limbs have been partially severed and thrown to the ground by strong winds, new root systems have developed and provided even more stability. The oldest tree has a five-metre girth.

One legend says that in AD859 a Viking raiding party returning to the coast through the valley was attacked by the men of Chichester and the ancient yews in the bottom of the valley were planted to commemorate the battle.

The old yews somehow managed to escape the fate which befell so many yew trees in the past. By the late 16th century the demand for yew wood to make long bows was so great that mature yew trees were almost extinct in northern Europe.

Today Kingley Vale is a nature reserve and is managed by Natural England using a combination of traditional methods. An hour-long nature trail starts at the valley bottom and takes you through the grove of ancient trees.

As you tread along its course you enter a strange spiritual world of weird sculptures in shady caverns. Shafts of sunlight light up the dark red and purple patterns on the smooth, strong limbs of the sleeping giants.

Naturalist WH. Hudson (1841-1922) writing about the trees said: "You may walk freely among the dark religious trees, with trunks like rudely fashioned pillars of red and purple iron-stone. One has the sensation of being in a vast cathedral, not like that of Chichester, but older and infinitely vaster, fuller of light and gloom and mystery and more wonderful in its associations."

As for the future, the yew forest will continue to develop and be carefully managed. One thing is sure, the yews, which have stood the test of time, will be there still.

The Bluebell Line

What better time to visit the Bluebell Railway than when the bluebells were in bloom! The sweet scent of the flowers mingled with the pungent aroma of wild garlic and, on the grass verges, tall buttercups swayed among the cow parsley. There were even a few primroses left. It was blooming lovely!

Cycle leaders, Ray and Jo led us on a merry ride through the undulating lanes of East Sussex to catch a glimpse of steam and hear the shrill sound of a whistle.

We took our bikes on a mainline train to Haywards Heath and we knew we'd have to catch an early train back. We couldn't risk the crush of rush hour. That could be a challenge for Ray and Jo whose rides tended to stretch out like elastic and fill the whole day.

From Haywards Heath station we cycled through Lindfield and took a track across a field of Friesian cows who stared mournfully through long lashes. We stopped in the Little Ritz café at Borde Hill Garden for coffee and tea cakes.

From there it was a short ride through leafy lanes, thick with hawthorn blossom, to Horsted Keynes railway station.

There was much to admire at the little red brick station; the stained glass windows in the porch, old luggage left in a heap in the waiting room, a map of old Sussex railway lines and Victorian postcards showing a different sort of seaside holiday in Sussex coastal towns.

And there were two Ladies Rooms with lavatories, (note the word use, not toilets) and polite notices about all sorts of things. Even the moustachioed ticket clerk, in smart uniform and cap, seemed to belong to another era. We wandered up the hill to a picnic area and ate our sandwiches, sharing a crust with a jackdaw.

There's something about steam, grit and the sound of an old locomotive that engenders a nostalgic sigh. We saw the steam rising in the distance and heard the train chug into the station. We couldn't see it so we climbed a high bank and watched as it pulled out.

The train emerged from the station and we looked down on another era; stately travel, no rushing, just ambling and taking time. We looked down and saw smiling faces at the windows, and in the locomotive, the fire raging, the fireman stoking and the steam rising and a pile of coal stacked high and ready.

We felt like the railway children, well almost, and we even raised a hand and gave a wave.

There was a short blast of the whistle and the train disappeared under the bridge and puffed away among the fields and hedgerows towards East Grinstead.

But we also had a train to catch. We cycled back past ponds and lakes and beech trees, freshly leafed and bright green, along the Sussex Border Path. We arrived at the station half an hour early. Ray had excelled himself, broken all previous records. Whatever next! Jo just smiled.

The Mappa Mundi

I have my very own Mappa Mundi. That ancient map of the world drawn in the 1300s has pride of place in my kitchen and when I'm flitting about drying the dishes, I can refer to it.

I like to see the river from hell which enters the sea boiling, cascading from the Umbrosi mountains, and the strange and wonderful creatures, one just like the Gruffalo, a bull with inward curving horns and a horse like mane.

Admittedly unlike the original in Hereford Cathedral, mine's not on a single piece of vellum (calf skin) drawn using pens from goose quill feathers, ink from oak apple gall and brushes from animal hair.

Mine is a tea towel "made with care in the UK of 100% cotton, colourfast, by Countryside Art" and bought in the cathedral gift shop. I was so entranced by the original map when I visited the cathedral recently that I had to have my own copy. There was so much detail that it was impossible to take it all in at once. It's the sort of map that you can keep looking at and see something new every time.

The original would have been vibrant with colour on the creamy white flesh side of calf skin. There would have been gold lettering and bright reds and blues.

Today it is somewhat faded but still in amazing condition considering it is 700 years old. My map is white and ocean blue with a numbered key and I can refer to it at any stage during the drying up process for a glimpse into the medieval view of the world.

The inhabited part of the world as it was known then, roughly equivalent to Europe, Asia and North Africa, is mapped within a Christian framework. Jerusalem is in the centre, and east is at the top and west at the bottom. East, where the sun rises, was where medieval Christians looked for the second coming of Christ. The British Isles is at the bottom on the left. Hereford is also on the map.

It can be a little confusing because it is more than a geographical illustration. As well as countries, towns and cities, it contains bible stories, myths and legends, beasts of the world both real and imaginary and some very strange people. It has 500 drawings and areas of text.

There are drawings of people with prominent lips with which they shade their faces from the sun, and the Sciapods who, though one legged, are extremely swift and they protect themselves from the sun by the soles of their feet. I like the idea of the Sciapods, dashing about on one leg but also the Blemmyes, a war-like race with no head and with their facial features in their chest.

My favourites are the Hyperboreans, a race who lived without discord and grief. In Greek mythology they lived in the far northern part of the world, a paradise of perpetual sunshine beyond the reach of the north wind. And they lived for as long as they wished but when they tired of living, they threw themselves into the sea from a prominent rock.

So, a lot to think about in my dish drying moments.

Houghton Mill

I walked down by the river at Houghton Mill and watched the meadow brown butterflies dancing in the long grass and the heron standing tall in the reeds and the iridescent blue damselflies, darting here and there. And I looked around, turning in every direction and saw only the river, the Great Ouse, flat fenland, trees and four church spires, a scene unchanged for centuries in this quiet corner of Cambridgeshire.

I had never seen four church spires in one sighting but I met a man later that morning who claimed to have seen at least ten. That was probably an understatement, he said.

There has been a water mill at Houghton in some form since 974 but then it would have been a rough hut, thatched with straw and owned by monks at a nearby abbey. The site was ideal for a water mill with an island forming a high point and a natural cataract in the long, lazy river, presumably called the Great Ouse because of the way it spilled over into adjoining meadows during heavy rainfall and floods.

It was early in the nineteenth century that the mill was extended and developed into the building you see today, a five-storey structure of brick with wood cladding. In its heyday it provided the best flour for the finest bakers in London.

Fire was a big risk for working mills because of the highly explosive concentration of flour dust and at least two mills on the site had burnt down.

The man responsible for the current mill's success was philanthropist and Quaker, Potto Brown. A bronze bust of him can be seen in the village square, on the corner, next to the antique shop where silver cake forks are still a popular purchase, and jugs and plates from every era decorate the shelves. And down the lane, pink and purple hollyhocks sway in the summer breeze outside beamed cottages. Houghton is a compact, pretty village and it is easy to imagine what life used to be like when Potto Brown ran the mill.

The grain arrived at the mill generally by barge and on a normal working day ten pairs of stones would grind one ton of grain per hour, about ten sacks. A horse drawn barge would carry the grain down the river to Kings Lynn and from there it would be transported south to the port of London for use in high quality bakeries.

Today the mill is owned by the National Trust and you can visit it and see the great cogs moving and watch the bags filling with flour, just as they did more than one hundred years ago.

I bought a bag of flour at the mill to make bread and scones. So now when I sit down at home, by the sea in West Sussex, and savour my bread, made from flour milled at Houghton, I can picture that idyllic scene and let my mind wander to the Great Ouse and the flat lands of the fens.

Another Wedding

The day starts dull, autumnal, blustery. Empty crisp packets billow along the breezy Wandsworth pavements, crinkly brown leaves gather in gutters and stick to wet tarmac. But the mood is far from dull.

Young Bertie arrives wearing a bow tie and braces and a bicycle helmet. He pushes smartly through the busy street, weaving in and out of the pedestrians on his scooter. We bump into Sarah, Clive, Owen and Harriet on a pedestrian crossing, smart wedding attire on top with comfy trainers and boots afoot. A woman waves and yells from a passing taxi that she'll see us soon. The wedding guests are emerging and converging.

At the Town Hall we wait in an anteroom with panelled walls and imposing interview style desk and heavy chairs. Owen, dark navy suit and pink tie, decides to take the chair and practise his interview skills, always important for an 11-year-old. But first he reminds us that pink, the pink of his tie, is the colour of friendship and love.

Bertie whisks along the corridor on his scooter. Simon and Ali and Bea sweep in behind him. Then the bride and groom pass by. We call and they turn and enter. There are long greetings and introductions, softly murmured for fear of disturbing an earlier ceremony taking place in the next room. The beautiful bride has a nervous, happy smile and the groom is proud and quite grown up now.

We are ushered in. The bespectacled registrar is a gentle man. He explains what will happen and he asks the vital question that could halt proceedings in an instant. "Does anyone know any reason why this couple should not be married?" No one speaks.

He tells us of things that we already know but are grateful for the reminder - that marriage needs honesty, patience and of course, a sense of humour. And it takes courage. So much courage.

'I'll be There for You' is the poem Sarah reads with the all-important message in the first line: 'I'll be there my darling through thick and thin.' Then there are vows about sharing and laughter and life-long love.

The wedding ceremony is over now. All the planning, smiles and tears and hard work is done. We're standing on the steps of the Town Hall. It's a casual group, not a formal bunched together, smiles set in concrete type of wedding picture. It's relaxed, happy, different.

The bridesmaids are in green – emerald, mint, forest, sea green, nothing matching in style or colour, but why should it. How can shades of green, nature's very own colours, not blend and mix and merge into a wonderful natural palette.

After a meal back at The County Arms where the air is abuzz with reunions and friendships old and new, there are speeches and declarations of love from the bride and groom. And the groom sheds tears, so many, that the guests laugh and cry too.

At the end of the evening when words are slurred and a bearded man is lurching like a sailing boat in a storm, from one side of the dance floor to the other, I bend down and pick up a single white rose attached to a pin, once a buttonhole, now abandoned to the sticky floor. I rescue it at midnight before the magic fades and the coach becomes a pumpkin and the silver slipper is lost. I wrap it in tissue paper and place it in my bag.

The next morning, I unfold the paper and place the rose in the palm of my hand. The petals are limp and edged with brown, like an old manuscript. The happy day is over, now just a memory. The sharp pin pricks my finger to remind me it was not a dream. In the end, when those fleeting moments of happiness pass, memories are all we have. And photos and words preserve the memory so that we can forever recall and relive, and keep alive that very special day.

Skiing or Cycling?

It wasn't the skiing holiday I'd planned. In fact, it wasn't a skiing holiday at all. I'd swapped a week's sliding down snowy slopes in the Dolomites for five days cycling in Hereford. I tried to convince myself that it would be similar. That I wouldn't miss the mountains. That I could give up skiing for good and settle for a more sedate old age pedalling through the British countryside.

Covid had scuppered my plans. I couldn't face being ill with Covid in an Italian hotel and not being allowed home so I'd cancelled the trip abroad and, feeling a great sense of holiday deprivation, opted for five days in the wilds of Hereford. In holiday deprivation mood, anything would do.

There were similarities of course. There were long down-hill stretches, free-wheeling through pine trees, cool fresh air filling my lungs, a beautiful sunset, a glorious feeling of exhaustion after a long day of exercise. But there were no lifts and the pleasure of free-wheeling only came after strenuous climbs up steep hills.

Temperatures were pretty similar, a piercing cold of just two degrees, on the first day when we set off at 9am. But there the similarities ended. The colour palette of the landscape was depressing. Where was the white sparkling landscape that lifts the spirits in the middle of the long winter gloom? Where was the blue sky? Just a mass of grey cloud, thick and low hovered over me.

It was as though I'd walked onto a child's magic slate where at the pull of a tab the whole picture had been wiped clean, leaving a blank grey space. I could still make out nearby trees but the distant hills had disappeared completely. The only white in the landscape were fuzzy puffs of old man's beard still clinging doggedly to hedgerows. It was a cold land, abandoned by the sun.

We did two thirty-mile circular cycling routes, one from Holme Lacy to Ross on Wye following the loops of the River Wye. Well that was what the cycle tour book said we'd do. The route would be basically flat with a few short sharp climbs. It was described as easy/moderate. We must have taken some wrong turnings because there were more than a few steep climbs and there was nothing basically flat about it.

We caught sight of the river briefly in the valley below soon after we started and then came along side it after 15 miles. The grey slab of water showed reflections of pine and beech reaching as deep into the river bed as the branches stretched high into the sky.

The other circular route from Ledbury to Bromyard started in cloud from the historic town of

Ledbury with its fine half-timbered houses and Market House. We had some good views of the Malvern hills and were assured by the cycling guide that we could admire them without climbing them and the route would again be easy to moderate. But you can't believe all you read in a guide book. I ended up walking up a couple of hills. One was so steep I had difficulty pushing my bike up it. We stopped in an old pub in Bromyard for lunch.

This was a brighter day and the sun came out in the afternoon and, like a spot light, showed up hedge rows sliced clean. Everywhere the countryside was neat and tidy in readiness for the coming season. There was a hint of lush summer harvests in the signs advertising plum and strawberry farms and there were rows of empty poles waiting for the new growth of hops. And in all the tall trees, branches were fat with baubles of mistletoe.

As we cycled back into Ledbury and the clock struck four, a piercing yellow glow of twilight was spreading across the sky and silhouetting trees on the nearby hills. Did that yellow glow compare with the pink splendour of a Dolomiti sunset over the mountains? Not quite but it was pretty spectacular. Will I swap my winter skiing holiday in Italy for a cycling trip in the UK? Not yet.

Australian Adventures

These start in Bondi with a competition winning piece about the early morning rituals on Bondi Beach and the remembrance of the Australian dead every evening at sunset. I still find it amazing that in the UK we have only one day of remembrance for the war dead. In Australia, throughout the country, at the Returned and Services Leave Clubs, they remember the war dead every evening at sunset.

On one of our trips to Australia, we drove up the east coast from Brisbane to Port Douglas. Australia makes great play of its deadly creatures and nowhere are you more aware of the risks than north of Rockhampton on the east coast where crocodiles, jelly fish and sharks all lurk. We heard tales of crocs being found on golf courses. There are warning signs by all the beaches to keep away from the shore because of the dangers.

It's a fascinating country but for me the wildlife proved pretty elusive as you will discover.

Bondi

It is 5.45 am and I emerge from my bed and breakfast accommodation. In the dim pre-dawn light a hooded figure slips silently by. He is barefoot and carries a large flat board under his arm. With head bowed he is walking purposefully. I close the door and follow. He pads down the main street under the fig trees, past a row of shops and cafes, not yet open.

The hooded man is gliding on and I quicken my pace. Already I can hear the sound of the ocean. We make our way down the stone steps, past the memorial to the Australian dead of two Worlds Wars, across the promenade and onto the soft sandy beach.

The surf is rolling in. Huge crashing waves thrust forward. The young man, now bare chested, is running down the beach, splashing through the waves and swimming out. The sea is studded with flotsam, as though a ship has been wrecked. I look again and realise that the black debris is scores of surfers waiting on their boards like praying mantises.

This is Bondi Beach, Australia. The air is still cool and as the sun rises the whole beach begins to move, gyrating and pumping in a fitness frenzy. A group of soft sand runners, the desert camels of Bondi, are ploughing deep in the sand, lifting feet high only to sink down again.

Other runners, sleek like panthers, are pacing along the promenade and, on the grass, under the Norfolk Island pines, muscles are expanding and contracting rhythmically in the green gym. In the pool at the southern end of the beach swimmers pound up and down in training. This is the other face of Bondi, one of Sydney's most fashionable beaches, which you have to rise early to witness.

As the sun rises and the rays strengthen, the intensity of activity fades and the beach takes on a relaxed, chilled out feel with bronzed bodies lazing in the heat

The evening rituals are quite different. The beach closes and, as the sun goes down, young and old retreat to their favourite bars for refreshment.

At the north end of the beach the surfers and sunbathers make for the RSL Club (Returned and Services League Club) for cheap beer and camaraderie. Every night at sundown the same ceremony takes place. The lights are dimmed and all are asked to stand and face west. Over the loudspeaker The Ode of Remembrance is read: "They shall grow not old, as we that are left grow old. Age shall not weary them, nor the years condemn. At the going down of the sun and in the morning, we will remember them."

There is a pause and then the words "Lest we forget". There was another sandy beach at Gallipoli, not unlike Bondi, where Australians soldiers fought for the freedom, the young people enjoy today. Remembering that sacrifice is not left to chance in Australia. There is a daily reminder, at sunset in Bondi and in RSL clubs throughout the land.

Was it a Pie Shop or a Pizza Shop?

We made two mistakes, arriving after dark and mixing up a pie shop with a pizza shop. We had taken the train from Sydney to Casino, near Brisbane, and then a country bus to Byron Bay. But the bus was late leaving. The driver spent ages ticking names off a long list and sorting the luggage meticulously by destination. Then he just gave up and flung the cases in randomly.

He wouldn't have been much good on the First Fleet, trying to get all those stallions and chickens and 500 women's petticoats into a sailing ship, I thought.

We set off and sped through dark, narrow roads, stopping in unlit towns to drop off passengers. We arrived in a car park at the railway station in Byron Bay. My husband grabbed his case and marched off through muddy puddles as if he knew where he was going.

"It's over the railway line," he said confidently.

There were lights in the main street of this sleepy East Coast beach town but beyond the station it was quite dark and we could see no way across the railway. It started to rain.

"There's a taxi," I said with relief, but, when we explained to the driver the address of our bed and breakfast, he said it would be easier to walk.

"Go along the main street as far as the pizza shop and turn right. A passageway will take you over the railway and the road you want is just opposite."

We walked back along the street but could see no pizza shop. Instead we came to a pie shop beside a dark alley.

"This must be it. He probably got his pies and pizzas mixed up," my husband said.

At the end of the alley the wire fence had been cut and bent back providing a way across the railway. On the other side there was another hole in the fence and in the dark, I could just make out, what looked like an animal track, through a field of shoulder high grass, beside a small river of shiny black water.

"I'll come back for you," he said and disappeared.

My case was not built for cross-country, no fat tyres or suspension. I lifted it and squelched through the wet grass, my feet scurrying on, lest something should creep from the undergrowth. Had we reached saltwater crocodile country yet? I couldn't visualise the East Coast map. Was this black water an estuary with crocs lurking? I hurried on waiting for the snap of teeth. At least I wouldn't need to do a night-time bush walk. Not after this!

We reached another unlit road and clutching a torch the size of a small cigar, tried to make out street names. After much stumbling and peering we managed to find our accommodation.

I thought about Captain Cook rounding the Cape Byron headland in the dark in 1770. The lighthouse was built there 130 years and many shipwrecks later. Maybe I needed to get a sense of proportion.

Crocodiles

We filed onto the flat-bottomed tin boat as it bobbed about on the crocodile infested Proserpine River in Australia. I was about to take a front seat when Scotty, our guide, warned: "Don't sit there. I forgot to mend the front seal and the boat is leaking. It's better if everyone sits further back."

"Don't worry, we won't sink," he reassured us. And then he added: "But if we do, we're very chivalrous here in Queensland. It's women and children first. Then once the feeding frenzy is over, we men can enter the water and wade safely to the bank."

Scotty laughed and the men on the boat laughed too. I knew this was Scotty's usual tourist patter but I shuddered at the use of the words "feeding frenzy". I glanced round and noted that fortunately there were several women on the boat fleshier than me.

We were advised not to lean out to take photographs or to let our arms dangle over the side of the boat.

"Be careful," Scotty said. "A croc can jump up and take a bird out of a tree."

They take crocodiles very seriously in this part of Australia. Most beaches north of Rockhampton on the east coast carry a warning sign.

"Keep well away from the water's edge and do not enter the water. Crocodiles inhabit this area and may cause injury or death." It's no wonder all those white sandy beaches and beautiful secluded bays are so empty.

The Proserpine River has the highest concentration of crocodiles on the east coast. It forms the northern boundary of the Goorganga wetlands, an Aboriginal term for a place of danger and evil spirits.

We drifted down the murky water on a falling tide, a cool breeze nudging the leaves of the mangroves and we listened to a thousand crocodile facts. Every floating log and tree stump looked ominous. Scotty, long hair tied back in a ponytail, and sporting a patch over one eye, was on the alert.

"They don't call me Hawkeye for nothing. I may only have one eye but I don't miss much."

We reached a bend in the river and we saw Ruby, an estuarine crocodile, sleek and muscular, sunning herself on the riverbank.

"She's a good mother." Scotty said.

Ruby would have laid up to 100 eggs and protected the nest for more than two months. She would have carried the young, 15 at a time, gently in her mouth down to the riverbank. There they risked being eaten by hawks and eagles or by fish. Only one per cent would survive to join the ranks of the world's greatest predator.

Ruby watched us for a while and then she slithered sideways over the mud into the river, one ton of flesh and bone, but like an Olympic diver, she disappeared beneath the surface without a single splash or ripple.

As we sat in our leaky boat, I did feel quite vulnerable but then Scotty revealed the most reassuring fact of the day. More people die every year in Australia, crushed by falling vending machines, than are killed by crocodiles. Apparently, people shake them when they fail to produce the wanted goods and the machines topple over. I glanced round. There wasn't a vending machine in sight.

A Precious Find Under the Water

Chairs were stacked on cafe tables, shops were shuttered, dry leaves rustled in the gutter. ANZAC day in Australia is a public holiday. Everything is closed until noon. Many towns and cities hold dawn services of commemoration.

At Port Douglas, where we were staying, the service was to be mid-morning but we had other plans. We were going on a fast catamaran to the Great Barrier Reef for a day of snorkelling.

We sat on deck opposite a young couple from Brisbane. She wore a straw hat over her dark brown hair. She could have been a tropical fish in her turquoise blue and pink striped bikini but there was warmth and love in her hazel eyes unlike the vacant stare of the underwater community. He towered above her, lean and gentle.

We were to snorkel in three different places on the reef. We donned our stinger suits, black Lycra from head to toe, to guard against the deadly jelly fish. The tall lanky Swedes, the Chinese family and the couple from Brisbane, we were all uniformly swathed. The young man seemed to be secreting something in the sleeve of his suit. His girlfriend was staring at the ocean.

We slithered off the back of the boat like seals slipping from the ice floe. We were having fun and they, the people of Port Douglas, would be marching down the main street now, towards the war memorial.

We hovered on the surface of the water, sky divers in free fall, wide eyed as hundreds of small fish crowded around us, brushing up against our legs with the gentle swish of a cat's tail.

We drifted over coral gardens of frilled lettuce, orange pumpkins and cream cauliflowers. Everything was quivering and fluttering. There was spaghetti and honeycomb, fungi, purple daisies on long green stalks, pink fingers pointing, great slabs of blue slate, sculptured and smoothed, a strange mix of shapes and colours. And everywhere the psychedelic dancers of the ocean were waltzing and twirling gracefully. We loitered, like humming birds drinking in the nectar.

We rose from the sea and clambered, dripping, onto the back of the boat, wriggling from our Lycra suits like butterflies emerging from chrysalises. There was a buzz of voices. Someone had seen a shark, someone else a turtle. Everyone shared their secrets from the deep.

Our young friends, now snug in hoodies, were smiling.

"What did you see"? I asked.

"I saw something absolutely brilliant," the young woman replied.

I waited and she remained silent. Then suddenly she thrust out her left hand and showed me that brilliant thing, a diamond ring, sparkling on her third finger. It had been an underwater proposal accepted with a spluttering seawater kiss. I shared a moment of celebration with strangers.

I thought about the people back in town. The service would be over now. The flowers, exotic orchids and chrysanthemums would rest at the foot of the memorial to the Australian war dead. And the message on them all: "Lest we forget." One young couple would not forget this day. Theirs would be a happy memory.

Batmen at the Opera

Large globules of rain hit the windscreen as our taxi pulled up at the entrance to Sydney's Botanical Gardens.

"A passing shower", the doorman said as he handed us plastic ponchos with our programme. "Just in case," he added. It had been one of Sydney's wettest summers but since our arrival the sun had shone and there was optimism about a warm, dry autumn.

We were to see La Traviata, Verdi's tragic love story, presented in the open air with a breath-taking backdrop of the Opera House and Sydney Harbour Bridge. The production had been billed as one of the greatest outdoor theatrical events this century. There were plans for it to become an annual event and to attract tourists from all over the world.

We made our way past the tiered seating and huge floating stage. A nine-metre high chandelier suspended over the stage was covered in thousands of crystals, more bling than in the firework display on the harbour bridge on New Year's Eve. The stage itself was a framed mirror floor secured by pylons drilled into the ocean bed.

We made for an open-air restaurant adjacent to the stage and sat on high stools. We ordered a simple pasta dish with pumpkin and spinach, and a glass of red wine. But as we sat admiring the harbour view and darkness fell, so did the rain. We put on our ponchos. The rain was falling heavily now and diluting my wine so I held my glass beneath my elegant plastic cape.

The volume of water increased and fell like a torrent down a mountainside. There was a risk that it would soon not just be the stage floating in the harbour. An official allowed us into a more select dining area which was under cover. We crowded together like ducks on the river bank, water dripping from our plastic feathers.

We had no qualms about our choice of fashion garment for the evening. Strangely everyone was wearing the same glamorous cape. Two men looked like professors at a graduation, their heads bowed as they spoke, their flowing capes became gowns over their dark grey suits. An elderly woman had tucked her poncho hood behind her ears and looked like a nun.

Then the sound and light show began. A blinding flash split the sky, lighting up the white shells of the opera house and the majestic metal structure of the bridge. A silver haired woman sitting nearby, silver bangles on her wrist, sparkled as the lightning shone on the water droplets on her cape. Another flash and crash, and all the lights went out. We waited and watched as the dramatic storm continued.

Then came the announcement: "The performance has been cancelled this evening because of the weather." Cancelled? We had already seen a spectacular show.

We stayed for a while until the son et lumière was almost over and then joined the trail of disappointed batmen, our plastic capes flowing, as we left the gardens.

Later when I studied the programme in more detail, I discovered that La Traviata is the only one of Verdi's operas to be set entirely indoors.

The Cassowary

I had not heard of the cassowary before I went to Australia and then, while I was there, I heard of nothing else. Like a poster for a wanted man, its face appeared in newspapers, on tourist brochures, even on a road sign.

This large flightless bird with its long, electric blue neck and haughty look, is an endangered species. It is also one of the world's most dangerous birds, capable of dealing a bone-breaking kick or a deep cut with its dagger like claws. It seemed to me more like a Lewis Carroll invention than a real bird and, like all Australian wildlife, it proved elusive.

I travelled over 1000 miles up the east coast from Sydney by train and road and I saw two dead kangaroos, a dozen ibis, a pelican in flight and a kookaburra, sitting in an old gum tree.

I saw many road signs warning me that there would be koalas for the next five kilometres or kangaroos at dawn and dusk. I saw notices about not going near the sea because of crocodiles and not swimming in the sea because of jellyfish with their 24 eyes and four brains. I heard about the blue-tongued lizard that lived under the sofa in our bed and breakfast.

On an evening sail, near Fraser Island, I saw the dark shadows of fruit bats as they returned from the island after supping from fruit trees. I was told that they hung around in trees in the local park during the day but in spite of an extensive search, I did not see any. Of course, there were some creatures I was grateful not to have seen but I didn't feel I could leave this vast, exotic continent without seeing at least one live kangaroo.

I reached Port Douglas and with three days of my holiday left, I decided on a visit to a wildlife habitat with its tasteful wetlands, grasslands and rainforest areas all enclosed in vast tents.

As I entered the habitat and stepped onto the boardwalk, I heard murmurings about the cassowary. I looked where everyone else was looking and could see nothing. Then I realised that it was hiding like a naughty boy in the corner. Its head was lowered with only its black rear protruding like a huge ball of knitting wool. It remained perfectly still, waiting for the onlookers to disperse.

I moved on. Long-legged curlews strutted like models on a catwalk, red-legged storks, stood together, hunched over, pondering serious matters, and fruit bats hung high in the trees like folding umbrellas.

I saw sleepy koalas, behaving like teenagers disturbed before noon, grunting and flickering an eyelid. I fed kangaroos, gentle, friendly creatures, standing piously with hands crossed and nibbling delicately from my hand, bristly chins tickling my palm. I stroked a snake and saw, close to, the blue fleshy tongue of the lizard that lived under sofas.

And then, as I walked round a corner, I came face to face with a cassowary. The punk of the bird world with its grey bony helmet, looked startled. This arrogant, beautiful creature, stared with disdain. I felt

like an uninvited guest at a party.

France by Bike

I love France and have had many holidays there over the years. More recently my holidays have been cycling tours. My first trip was Cycling to Paris and that piece of writing also won the weekly Telegraph travel competition. By the way I think Trevor still has his dried pasta ready for another excursion. Maybe he's waiting for a chance to take it back to Paris.

Cycling the D-day beaches was a moving experience and another prize-winning piece. On a different trip we visited the American landing beaches and, seeing the terrain, looking over the steep cliffs which the soldiers scaled and then visiting the cemetery with the endless rows of white crosses. was quite disturbing.

From a cycling perspective, finding La Velodyssee, the south west cycle route from Biarritz to the Loire, was a stroke of luck. Just before we set off to cycle from Biarritz to St Malo, Michael (He had no Soles) discovered a book about the route quite by chance in a book shop in Biarritz and as a result our tour was made far easier and mostly off road.

Cycling to Paris

Gerry is the pacemaker and Trevor, the snail. Trevor carries the contents of his house on his bike, and is a little slow on the hills. He has brought with him a colourful array of jackets and tops, two pairs of shoes, a complete pharmacy, as well as camping equipment and food. His dried pasta with cheese is making its second cycling trip to Paris in eight months.

Trevor comes from the windswept hills of North Wales. He is my saviour. With three younger, more experienced touring cyclists in the group I expected to be left behind, gasping for breath, lost forever in the French countryside. But although Trevor's pedals revolve faster than a hamster on a wheel, I can glide up the hills past him.

We are cycling from Dieppe to Paris and back to Le Havre. There are four of us, two campers and two less hardy folk. I am one of the hotel softies. I want the luxury of a comfy bed, clean sheets and hot shower.

There are other differences too. The campers are stuck in English time. I have moved forward an hour. There are several occasions when meeting up requires a little clarification. If we arrange to meet at 9.15, Trevor complains: "That means we've got to get up at 7.15 English time.

From Dieppe we make for the Avenue Verte and cycle along smooth paths, meadows on either side, Charolais cows lying under trees, apple orchards in full blossom, sheep grazing and cocks crowing.

On the third day we cycle into Paris and into springtime magic, through the Bois de Boulogne, people walking, running, cycling, the horse chestnut trees laden with blossom. At the Arc de Triomphe mad drivers join the vast roundabout at speed. Gerry crosses to the centre. Miraculously he survives. The rest of us slink round the edges, heads swivelling nervously. Then we cycle triumphantly down the Champs-Élysées.

We ride beside the churning River Seine, water spilling onto the quayside. We visit Notre Dame and then cross to the Left Bank, past the golden dome of Les Invalides and on to the Eiffel Tower, its great girders submerged at the base in a sea of purple blossom.

We leave Paris in sunshine, and cycle on for three dull, grey days. We climb onto a high plateau, bleak and treeless, wheat and rapeseed fields for miles and battle on in drizzle against a strong headwind.

On the final day we follow our breath into an icy breeze towards the coast. We tight rope cycle over the great Normandy Bridge and then fight off the monsters of the road, juggernauts roaring towards the port of Le Havre.

We rest on the ferry and watch a non-horizontal horizon. The boat is listing because it has been badly loaded. Or is it something to do with the weight of Trevor's bike? He still had his dried pasta and cheese with him. Will his pasta be making a third cycling trip to Paris?" I wonder.

American Beaches in Normandy

The white-haired man stood in shorts and sandals, his face smudged with tears, his lips mouthing the words of the American national anthem as it rung out across the cemetery. Tourists stopped, stood erect, some placed hand on heart. The stars and stripes of the American flag flew stiff like cardboard in the breeze.

More than 9,000 white crosses patterned the grass of this beautiful stretch of land by the sea at Colleville-sur-Mer, the American Cemetery in Normandy, France. Pink lilies floated on a pool of black water stretching out from a giant bronze statue symbolizing the spirit of American youth rising from the waves.

'Mine eyes have seen the glory of the coming of the Lord' were the words on the memorial. We'd looked into the eyes of the soldiers, crammed together in the landing craft. They were there on film and in photographs in the museum. One survivor had written: "As the boat touched sand and the ramp went down, I became a visitor to hell."

It had been a grey day in every sense of the word. We had cycled under heavy cloud down the eastern side of the Cherbourg peninsula towards the D-day beaches.

We'd stopped at the Pointe du Hoc, the highest point between the two American beaches, Utah and Omaha and we'd trudged the grey gravel path to the edge of the 100 foot-cliffs and looked down at the grey flat sea, to the beach where the American Rangers had landed on 6th June.

The only sound, a swishing of waves breaking on the shore; a hushed landscape, swarming with silent visitors, trailing over the dips and hollows, climbing into bunkers and gun emplacements, breathless with the magnitude of the task undertaken more than 70 years ago.

The climb looked impossible, sheer cliffs of yellow sandstone. But the rangers used ladders and ropes with grappling hooks and many used bayonets or knives, any means possible to fasten themselves to the vertical surface and to enable them to climb, to make their way to the top and at the same time dodge the gunfire of the enemy.

They scaled the cliffs. They seized the German artillery so hazardous to the landings on Omaha and Utah beaches and they held on against fierce attacks. And by seizing the land at the top of the cliffs, they were part of the force that took back Europe. After two days of fighting only 90 of the 250 Rangers were still standing.

This bleak inhospitable landscape is still scarred today, a moonscape of craters, now grass covered and with brown sheep grazing.

As I cycled on towards Gold beach, I hummed the tune of the American national anthem and the words came to me, the last two lines, the words the man had been struggling to sing at the cemetery.

O say, does that star-spangled banner yet wave
O'er the land of the free and the home of the brave?

Yes, the American flag was still flying at the cemetery and from hundreds of houses along the way.

D- Day Landing Beaches in the 21st Century

We emerged from the 360-degree film of the D-day landings, deaf from the noise of gun fire and giddy from the spiralling rows of white crosses in the cemeteries.

We rolled our bikes down the steep path to Arromanches, on the Normandy coast of France and stopped at a café for lunch and a cool beer. The great grey slabs of the Mulberry Harbour were being battered by the waves. In the sea a young girl was fighting with a large inflated shark; on the beach, holiday-makers were enjoying the warm sun. On the promenade a young boy sat in a miniature bi-plane, flying round among the giraffes and galloping horses on the carousel. These were the D-day landing beaches more than 70 years later.

The wind had been sharp in our faces as we cycled the 20 miles from Ouistreham to Arromanches. To travel by bicycle was to see many memorials only visible from the coastal path and to get a real feel for the terrain and difficulties facing the allies on 6 June 1944. Every small town and village had erected a memorial and plaque recording a different incident from that historic day. Everywhere flags fluttered.

At St Bernières-sur-Mer we saw the first house to be liberated by seaborne forces, the men of the Queen's Own Rifles of Canada. More than 100 of them were killed or wounded in the first few minutes of the landing. Nearby was a picture of the house at the time, standing alone on the seafront and surrounded by a mass of soldiers and tanks. Today a plaque records the details of that day and the memorial is covered with crosses, flowers and poppies.

We stopped and viewed Cosy's bunker, named, not for its warmth and homeliness but after Sgt Cosy, a Canadian soldier entrusted with the mission of capturing the German pillbox at Graye-sur-Mer, with 15 men from the B company of the Royal Winnipeg Rifles. They succeeded but Sgt Cosy was hit in the chest. Today life-sized metal silhouettes of fighting soldiers lurk among the tall grasses in the sand dunes.

We left the coastal path and ventured up the hill to the village of Ver. From there we could look across the meadows of creamy Charolais cattle to the wild sea beyond. There were real poppies growing among the ripening corn. This would have been a good vantage point for the enemy and a vulnerable position for the young Canadians wading ashore.

We cycled back to Ouistreham to board the ferry home. As we waited at the terminal, we chatted to a young couple who had been cycling in the area. The young woman stood astride her bicycle, blonde hair drifting in the sea breeze, and dismissed the memorials to the dead in one flippant comment: "They don't half milk the D-day landings in this area," she said, smiling.

Overhead a gull's cry seemed to echo the pain of millions.

He Had No Soles

Michael had a problem with his shoes, his evening shoes to be precise. It may seem strange taking evening shoes on a cycling holiday but we didn't feel we could tip-tap round the restaurants of west coast France in cycling shoes so, at Michael's suggestion, we had all packed a 'going out' pair.

Mine were flat and sensible; nothing sequined or ostentatious. Michael's were brown leather, polished and shiny on top, a little ragged underneath. "Why," he asked "Would I take my best shoes on a cycling holiday to cram into panniers?

We were cycling from Biarritz through the pine forests and sand dunes of Les Landes, north to the Loire and finally to St Malo on the north coast, a 600-mile trek over two weeks. Lots of pedalling by day and a lot of eating out by night.

Les Landes, where once the shepherds walked on stilts tending their sheep on the marshy land, have today been planted with thousands of maritime pine, tall leggy trees with a flourish of needles like curly top knots.

Apart from the trees, there were other interesting specimens; clusters of slim, strong bodies, swathed in black rubber, idling on the board walks, some only half clad with long black uninhabited rubber arms, stretching down to their ankles. Surf boards leaning against cars. Casual was the look in this surfing paradise. Shoes, no shoes, it didn't matter. The term flip flop took on a whole new meaning in Michael's case.

On our first night by the silver lake at Léon, Michael mentioned a slight floppiness of sole as we ambled to a lakeside restaurant where we feasted on ducks' hearts and moules.

At Arés it was wet underfoot on the gritty path to the restaurant. Michael was concerned that the rain would seep in but he didn't need to worry. His shoes were now self-draining. For the next few evenings our choice of restaurants was limited to those within shuffling distance.

We had decided on a rest day at La Rochelle. We will remember the city for its turbulent history and beautiful buildings but Michael will recall it as the day he lost his soles to a French cobbler, an attractive young woman in a leather apron with no heart. Only soles. She looked at Michael's shoes. She turned them over and with a sharp flick of the wrist she removed the soles.

"Caput," she said, handing back the shoes. "You need to go and buy some new ones."

"Please can I have my soles back," Michael asked. So clutching his shoes, now in four parts, he walked barefoot back to the hotel.

For the rest of the holiday he padded about like a man in slippers, just a thin slice of leather between him and the ground. On the ferry back to Portsmouth he examined his shoes. "I'll get the soles stuck on when I get home and they'll do for next year's trip.

Marseille to Barcelona

The Spanish sun was beating down but I kept pedalling. Struggling up the steep hill in the Pyrenees I could feel my heart pounding and my face burning with exertion. I was determined to get over the pass and down to the sandy beaches of the Costa Brava.

I could hear the purr of the idling engine of the support van behind, waiting for me to falter so it could scoop me up and whisk me to the top of the hill. I didn't want to give in.

I'd joined the cycling group knowing I might be last but was relieved there was an 80-year-old with us. But he had taken the e-bike option and powered up the hills past even the strongest cyclists.

"We will go at the speed of the slowest," Gregorio, our Spanish leader declared on day one of our cycling trip from Marseille to Barcelona, before we'd even pressed foot to pedal.

Gregorio looked more matador than cyclist - an imposing man, tall and imperious, encased in lime green Lycra shorts and crimson top, his long hair coiled by day and falling to his waist at night. Matador in stature only. There was no swirling cape, no black hat and no bull.

We didn't go at the speed of the slowest. An athletic Canadian swept ahead the whole way, pulling us forward.

It was fine in the flat country of the Camargue where the land seemed to drop away and we wondered if we might fall off the edge, and where lakes were filled with flamingos in fifty shades of pink.

It was fine on the coastal tracks, by sand dunes and pine forests, by the rice fields and vine yards.

It was fine until we arrived at the big hills. Even then it was fine to start with, just a gradual climb past prickly cacti, gazing with their flat prickly faces and waving their flat prickly hands.

The hill steepened. I tried to distract myself, searching the slopes for cork oaks and strawberry trees. Suddenly speeding towards me came the matador. I ignored him. He turned and came alongside me.

"Would you like to make your life easier? You can go in the van you know?"

He was cajoling, tempting, softening his voice, but I didn't want to give in.

"I'll keep going," I said. "Slowly."

"That is not a problem. You can go as slowly as you like." I was reassured, momentarily.

"I have to tell you there's still two kilometres to go and it gets steeper, and three of our group are already at the top."

"OK I give in."

It was like a pincer movement, the matador moved sideways, the truck overtook and moved in front, the back doors opened, my bike was slung inside and I climbed in beside the driver. Capitulation!

At the top I glanced at my exhausted friends. I could see the Mediterranean in the distance. I climbed back on my bike and began the long freewheel descent to the sea.

Edge of the Land

We were planning to go to the edge of the land, to a promontory where the sea brushed the rose granite. We'd seen a plastic place mat on a newsagent's stand with a picture postcard view of the ragged coast with its small rocky islands and pine tree silhouettes under a cloudless blue sky.

"It'll be great," the others said, still brimming with energy at the end of a hard day's cycling. But on a bicycle no one takes lightly a decision to make an eight-mile detour. Not at the end of the day. Not when the light is fading and a fine drizzle is falling from a grey sky.

We were spending a week cycling in Brittany, France. In the first few days, on our excursion south, we saw more cows than people. Herds of black-eyed beasts roused themselves, wandered to the fence and stared as we cycled past, as if we were the most exciting thing they'd seen all day. Certainly, the feeling was mutual.

There was an autumnal stillness about the place and in the fields and hedgerows reminders of summer, odd flashes of pink clover, red apples on trees and orange pumpkin lying on the earth, startlingly bright as if already lit for Halloween.

Now we were back by the sea and the ragged coast required choices - to go to the headland and see the view or to take a short cut and miss it. A cyclist must enjoy the journey as well as the destination but the pleasure gained should be directly related to the effort involved.

"Come on," they said. "You saw the picture. It'll be beautiful."

I wasn't convinced. In fact, I was sceptical. Ernest Renan, that famous French writer and sceptic, whose statue we had stopped and admired earlier in the day in Tréguier, had affected my thinking. His quote: "Oh God, if there is a god, save my soul if I have a soul" had morphed into: "Oh God, not all that pedalling to see a view that may be obliterated by mist."

So we parted company. They struck out for the headland. I made for the town. I watched as they disappeared along the narrow country lane between fields of maize. I sliced across the promontory and headed for the hotel, a warm shower and a glass of wine in the bar overlooking the harbour.

Later after I had sat silently munching a mountain of mussels and listened to much eulogising about the marvellous views I had missed, how easy the cycling had been, how they were there and back in a flash, I decided to ask for evidence.

Michael produced his camera. "It's a panoramic shot," he said. And then by way of apology: "Not quite as good as the placemat."

I took the camera. "But it's nothing like the placemat," I replied. "It's just a few greenish shadows on a grey sea. Definitely not worth the effort." Thank you, Monsieur Renan, for that moment of scepticism.

Wildlife

I stared into the elephant's squinting eye. It was not the wildlife encounter I had expected, not on a cycling holiday in France. I'd seen a dead fox and a cormorant juggling and swallowing an eel the size of a cobra.

And two members of our group returned from an exploration to the upper reaches of the River Rance with tales of camel and lion sightings. Now elephants in a field by the side of road. That was a little strange.

We stopped to talk to the elephants but they were far too busy grazing; hoovering up clumps of dry grass with their trunks and stuffing it into their mouths. They were refuelling for their next circus act.

It occurred to me that we cyclists had a lot in common with the elephants. We had been grazing too, refuelling as we travelled from Caen to St Malo and up the peninsula to Cherbourg.

We'd halted at the top of a steep hill and collapsed under a crucifix to eat dry bread and biscuits. In monsoon conditions we'd sheltered in a tunnel on a disused railway track and crunched our way through oat and nut bars. On the quayside of a fishing village, we'd picnicked on French bread and cheese.

Grazing had become a necessity in the barren Normandy countryside. Where were the cafés to provide nourishment for hungry cyclists? We'd glimpse a church spire in the distance and our tummies would rumble in anticipation of a village cafe but when we arrived, we would find only spiritual sustenance. No coffee cup the size of a soup bowl and no warm croissant to dangle in it.

We cycled on past endless fields of maize, emerald tongues lolling in the sunshine, glistening and shiny in the rain and flailing wildly in the wind, the fat cobs still not quite ripe. And with our minds distracted with thoughts of food we pondered at length the all-important question - where do cornflakes come from?

By dusk we were tired of grazing. We sought the true French culinary experience, a country restaurant with net curtains and flies and all-inclusive four course menus. But we were staying in cheap hotels on out-of-town commercial centres and after cycling 60 miles no one had the energy for the extra two-mile push into town for dinner. Instead, we ate in concrete warehouses masquerading as restaurants.

And in the morning, we climbed into showers still hot and steamy from the previous occupants and then queued for breakfast in cramped dining areas. No waking to the aroma of fresh bread and coffee brewing, and to the sound of a church clock chiming.

Where was the real France? On the last night we found a traditional French restaurant and consumed mussels and frites and crème brûlée and small quantities of wine poured from blue bottles. The men lapsed into technobabble and lulled us with talk of sprockets and noodles until our eyes glazed over. I went to bed and dreamed of cycling with elephants.

Monet's Garden

A woman strayed off the gravel path and was immediately brought to a halt by a shrill blast on a whistle. The official waved his arm and pointed, demanding that she retreat to the public area. We stared as she hastened back to the path. She had dared to venture beyond the metal chain, a chain that ensured there was one vista in Claude Monet's gardens at Giverny, France, completely free of people.

There are times when I hate being a tourist and times when I become irrationally intolerant of other tourists. I wanted the gardens empty so that I could enjoy them quietly. No crunch of a hundred feet on gravel, no clicking of cameras or murmurings of wonder. No blemish on an otherwise perfect scene.

I had cycled to Giverny from Paris, along country lanes with views of the river, lilac spilling over old stone walls and iris blurring the edges of the road. I had taken a detour to visit Monet's garden, a detour which by car would be quite insignificant but by bike required energy and determination.

I stayed in an old converted water mill by the main road where water tumbled day and night, and where, strangely, ostriches and wallabies roamed in the grounds. I left my sunflower room of yellow chintz and creaking floorboards early so that I could beat the crowds pouring out of Paris by coach. But when I reached the gardens, I realised that everyone else had had the same idea.

Inside the gardens, I joined the slow march along the network of gravelled paths. I marvelled at the tulips, fluted, frayed and frilly, colours straight from an artist's palette. I loved the haze of forget-me-nots. I sauntered behind the young, the old and the infirm, all travelling at the same slow pace, all stopping to take pictures and block the pathways.

I wandered through the underpass to the lily pond. There, surely, I would find some seclusion and peace, the soft greens and blues of Monet's pictures, the Japanese bridge, willow draping in still waters. But to my dismay a stagnant queue of people stretched round the circumference of the lake.

The view to the other side, to the bridge, framed with purple wisteria, was of more people loitering. And, in the lake, under the water lilies, were the reflections of people standing upside down in their multi coloured jackets, a kaleidoscope of colour under the dull green leaves.

I made a hasty retreat, climbed on my bike and pedalled away. I breathed the sweet air of the countryside and swept past trees laden with apple blossom and grass verges spun with cow parsley.

The next day I arrived in Le Havre for the ferry with time to spare so I visited the modern art museum on the seafront. Inside I found Monet's painting of the River Seine at Vétheuil. It was in delicate greens and blues, still water, tall trees, reflections. And not a tourist to be seen anywhere.

France –

Apples, Artists and Wine

These are a collection of random tales from several holidays in France but mainly from post-retirement volunteering on French farms and small holdings.

Christian Encounter was strange and like all my stories, completely true, but a great example of how the oddest things happen in the most ordinary settings.

There are two pieces about Van Gogh. I really enjoyed walking in the footsteps of Van Gogh in St Remy de Provence where he spent a year in the asylum, and also in Auvers Sur Oise where he spent the last month of his life before he committed suicide. The visit to the cemetery to see the graves of Vincent and his brother Theo was a poignant moment.

Three out of the four wine tales are set in Macon where our good friends Bob and Liz have a share in a vineyard and have invited us to stay on many occasions. We've been on numerous wine tasting visits with them and each one has been an 'experience'.

Apple Picking in Normandy

A rumble like distant thunder and the apples tumble to the ground. We fall to our knees like priests at prayer. All around us, little orbs of gold, la Douce Moen, an apple that looks more like an apricot, a soft orange colour tinged with rose. I taste one. It is sweet and floury. It will be used for cider, not juice.

It is apple picking time in the orchards of Normandy, France, and I have volunteered to spend a month working on an organic farm. The warm autumn days make me feel that summer is not yet over, even though it is already November.

The striker goes ahead with a long pole, shaking the trees and knocking down the apples. We follow on hands and knees, filling buckets and sacks with the sweet gems. We scramble and scratch in the long grass like dogs searching for bones. I think Pierre was a dog in a previous life. He burrows deep and emerges clutching handfuls of apples and looking pleased with himself. I resist the temptation to pat his head.

One thousand trees, standing tall in neat rows. Five different varieties of apple, some better for juice and other more suitable for cider. All organic. "It is fundamental to live in harmony with nature," says Veronique, the farmer, a steely look in her dark eyes.

89

"One must always think of the consequences of one's actions," she adds. Her hands are black like her hair. They are stained with the juice of the apples which rule her life. Her back is broad and she can lift a sack of apples with one hand.

All around us we hear nature's melodies, the braying of the donkeys in the adjoining field, the singing stream, the soothing breath of the wind in the poplars and the cackle of guinea fowl on a distant farm, laughing at an interminable joke. In the orchard the chattering French voices of students, teachers and local farmers, all volunteers who have turned out to lend a hand. And all the time the thud, thud of apples falling into buckets.

At 12.30 we go to the farm house for a lunch of galettes, salad and tarte Normande which we eat at long tables in the courtyard. The cats hang around like a gang of thieves, waiting for their chance to pounce and steal from our plates.

We return to the orchard and work late into the afternoon. When we walk back to the farmhouse weary and warm, the crescent moon is already up. We stand on the terrace and drink tea and apple juice and eat slices of a spicy cake made by a local artisan until the moon is high in the sky and the air is quite chilled. A barn owl screeches. I breathe deeply and feel the ache in my back. I yearn to soak in a hot bath, lit by candles and sipping Calvados. Is that what they mean by living in harmony with nature, I wonder.

Christian Meeting

I met some Christians on my way to Nimes. I had been staying in a remote farmhouse in the depth of the Cevennes Mountains in southern France and my host had agreed to drop me at a bus stop in the nearest town so that I could spend a day in the ancient Roman city.

It was dark and wet at 7am when I joined three young women already waiting for the bus, one with a large suitcase. English words floated in the air so I enquired

"Are you English?" The reply was not unlike the opening of a television game show.

"I'm Kathy, I'm from Chile," said the shortest of the three.

"I'm Melodie, I'm French," said the tallest, curls piled high on top on her head.

"I'm Alicia, I'm from Germany," said the medium sized blonde girl.

And then came words, probably never previously heard on that type of programme. "We're Christian missionaries." Halos of moisture hung in the dank morning air.

I questioned the demand for conversions in southern France. "It's more about telling people about our love of Jesus," Kathy explained. "Do you pray to Jesus?" she asked.

I'd got up at 5.30 and I was concentrating on my physical rather than spiritual journey. I was looking forward to a day in a busy city as an antidote to the silence of the dark forests. I wasn't prepared for searching questions. But I scraped the bottom of my soul for remnants of latent Christianity and then in a very un-Christian like manner, I moulded the truth. "In my own way," I declared.

"Then shall we say a pray together?" Melodie suggested. So we huddled together and Melodie prayed for Alicia's safe journey to Germany and for me, to find continuing strength in Jesus. We all said "Amen" and then in a flash of lights and a splash of puddles, the bus arrived. My new friends hugged me like old friends, Alicia and I climbed aboard and were whisked away.

By the time the bus arrived in Nimes, the day had dawned, the rain had cleared and warm southern sun lit the white stone buildings. I spent the morning at the Roman arena and heard tales of its bloody past; of Christians being thrown to lions and gladiatorial contests. The sandy surface was regularly raked to hide the smell and sight of blood. It is still used today for bull fighting.

At lunchtime I sat in a café in the forum and heard the beating of drums, feet marching and voices raised in chant. Hundreds of people appeared in the square carrying banners and shouting "Say no to bull fighting." Police vans and cars spilled men on to the streets. A woman took a megaphone and condemned cruelty to animals.

Nimes, it seems, has always had a taste for blood. At least they don't throw Christians to the lions any more. There has been some progress but maybe a little missionary work would not be wasted.

On the Bridge at Avignon

There are three children on the bridge in Avignon today. But they are not dancing. They are looking thoroughly bored. Their parents are giving them a history lesson. The middle-sized child, probably only six years old, is standing defiantly with her hands on her hips and lips in full pout. No coaxing can persuade her to listen to a recorded commentary on the history of the bridge.

She has been lured there by the children's song, 'Sur le Pont d'Avignon'. I heard her humming it. At the entrance gate she would have seen the picture of children dancing, holding hands in a ring, flowers and ribbons in their hair, the girls wearing full red skirts and ballet pumps, and the boys, knee length breeches.

She is expecting more than a walkway of brown cobbles, a small chapel and four arches. The bridge doesn't even span the whole river.

I leave the family and stroll along this famous bridge and learn that people used to picnic on the island in the river and there were cafes and open-air dance halls under the bridge. That was where they danced, under it, not on it.

Late October is a good time to visit Avignon. It is warm but not too hot, quiet and without the crush of tourists.

After the bridge, I make for the Palace of the Popes. I spend the afternoon wandering through vast, empty rooms and towers, listening to stories about this French papal city.

I get up early the next morning. I am due to fly home and I want to visit the terraced gardens of the Rocher des Doms, perched on a cliff above the Rhone.

I open my shutters and the city is veiled in mist. I climb the long flight of stone steps, past the cathedral, and walk up the slope towards the gardens. I hear the drone of a mowing machine and ducks laughing wildly.

I never reach the gardens. I am drawn to a large stone plaque on one of the garden walls. It contains the names of 300 Jewish men, women and children from the region, the Vaucluse, who deported to Nazi extermination camps. Fifty-four were children. The adults' names are written in black and the children's names in white. There is a cross by the side of those who survived. Fewer than 30 adults returned and only two children. Sylvain three months, Ellen, aged 8, and Maria, 11, are among those who never came back. I spend ages reading the inscriptions.

A clock chimes the hour and reminds me that I have a plane to catch. I walk back into the square. A girl is skipping away from the palace towards the bridge holding her parents' hands. She is singing in a high-pitched, sweet voice, Sur le Pont d'Avignon.

I think of the Jewish children who did not return to the city. They have had no chance to sing or dance on the bridge. Or even to be bored with tales of its past.

Bertie and the Maze

"It's alright. We won't get lost," young Bertie assured me as we entered the maze. He spoke confidently with the air of an explorer. He hurried on. A born leader, I thought. His straw hat firmly in place, he looked as though he had emerged from the African bush early in the last century.

It was a maize maze, thick and dry and brittle at summer's end. And tall, at least seven feet, so no chance of peering over the top and even less chance of little Bertie taking a bearing from above.

On we went. Bertie in front, pattering along, and me, following closely, not wanting to get left behind

We were staying in the Lot and Garonne area of south west France, the orchard of Europe where plum trees grow, row upon row in huge forests. And field upon field of maize sprouts with brown, bearded fat corn, and acres of sunflowers flourish, now looking a little sad, their yellow petals shrunk and black faces staring down like priests at prayer, their daily search for the sun over.

The maze was the highlight of the afternoon for Bertie. Not surprisingly he had not been captivated by the history of the shrivelled plum. We'd spent almost an hour in a prune museum, poking our heads into ancient ovens and admiring drying racks and old posters promoting the medicinal values of the prune's purgation properties.

We'd tasted prunes coated in sugar and chocolate, and prunes soaked in whisky and eau de vie, a fire water so strong that even in the maze I could feel its fiery effect at the back of my throat.

Bertie led me to the centre where a high wooden gantry gave us a view of the whole maze. We clambered up the rickety steps and stared out over the vast sea of what looked like crinkly brown paper.

Unable to memorize at a glance the intricacies of the passageways, we went back down and ambled on. We trod the cement-like earth which offered no clues. There were no shoe indents to help us retrace our steps. Oh for a trail of breadcrumbs or even prunes. We came to a junction.

"Now which way?" I asked.

"Just follow me," Bertie declared. And he set off purposefully. We came to several signs where he paused and seemed to study the instructions even though his three short years on this earth had neither equipped him with the ability to read nor interpret the French language.

"This way," he said, after a little deliberation. I followed him, turning left and right and left again as he decreed. The sun beat down and I feared we would be lost forever among the corn with only a few yellow niblets to sustain us.

Miraculously we took another left turn and emerged from the maze. We'd escaped. "Thank you, Bertie. How ever did you do it?" Saved by a three-year-old boy with the homing instinct of a pigeon.

In the Footsteps of Van Gogh

I went to St Rémy, France, for a friend's birthday celebration but I was drawn into an artist's world. St Rémy was home to Vincent Van Gogh for just one year when, because of his fragile mental state, he was admitted to the St Paul de Mausole asylum in May 1889. But In spite of his mental instability, it was probably the most prolific period in his ten-year career and he produced more than 140 paintings.

The asylum is on the outskirts of the small Provencal town in southern France at the foot of the great white rocks of the Alpilles range. The town is attractive with its narrow streets and square, shaded with plane trees.

The chapel bells were ringing as I walked down the avenue of pines towards the tall stone walls and gates of the asylum. Olive trees, leaves pale grey-green, trunks black and twisted, filled the fields on either side. Wild thyme cast a mauve hue over the grass.

I was entering Van Gogh's world. It was as though I had been there before. Van Gogh painted these scenes more than 100 years ago but they have changed little and seemed strangely familiar. The images of his pictures were all around. It was like walking in a living exhibition of his work. I saw his paintings in the black cypress trees, the bright yellow fields of wheat, in the white rocks, the twisting bending olive trees, yellow skies and violet earth.

I met my guide, Marie Charlotte, at the entrance to the asylum, and she took me into the olive grove. She held up one of Van Gogh's pictures of olive trees and, behind her diminutive figure, I saw the same view. She showed me other reproductions of Van Gogh's paintings. I glanced from picture to the countryside around me and back to picture. Everywhere I saw the reality of his paintings.

Van Gogh found respite and relief in interaction with nature. When he painted the series of olive tree paintings, he was ill and in emotional turmoil, yet the paintings are among his finest work.

He found the trees both demanding and compelling. "The wind blows and I see the waves sweep through the branches." he told his brother, Theo. He said that he was struggling to catch the olive trees. He found the rustle of the olive grove had something very secret in it. "It is too beautiful for us to dare to paint it or be able to imagine it."

Marie Charlotte took me on a tour of the asylum, the cloisters and chapter house. In the entrance hall I turned and looked back at the door. This was another of his pictures. Van Gogh had two small rooms, one a bedroom and the other, a studio. I saw a room similar to the one he used, with the iron bed and rush-seated chair.

I saw the view from his bedroom window, from which he did a series of paintings recording the changing seasons. I walked out into the walled garden where he walked and where he painted irises, lilacs, and ivy-covered trees. I ambled among long rows of lavender, past persimmon trees, the oozing orange flesh of the fruit squashed into the dry mud.

"I put my heart and my soul into my work and have lost my mind in the process," Van Gogh wrote to his brother, Theo.

When Van Gogh arrived at St Remy he was on the road out of melancholy. When he left one year later, the medical report said "cured". A month later he died from a gunshot wound, generally accepted to be self-inflicted although no gun was ever found. He was 37. He had sold just one painting during his life.

Van Gogh's Final Days

Two small white headstones stand against a rough stone wall in the hill top graveyard at Auvers-sur-Oise, 30 miles from Paris. A tangle of ivy weaves a dark tapestry over the ground.

To one side, sunflowers, entwined in the stem of a pale pink rose, nod over the graves. I turn and look back across the countryside, down to the village which is submerged in a canopy of green leaves. The view is lush and peaceful. A cock crows.

Vincent and his brother, Theo, would have liked this final resting place, up here together, among the wheat fields.

Van Gogh spent the last days of his life in Auvers. He did not want to stay in Paris. He loved the countryside and wanted to be outside, working in the fresh air. In 70 days, he completed 70 paintings.

To walk round the village and surrounding fields is to walk where he walked and to see the scenes he painted. All the scenes are familiar, the gardens, the wheat fields, the houses and the church.

As I leave the graveyard and walk back down the hill, I come to the church, stark and grey, like the upturned hull of a boat. On a board outside is a reproduction of Van Gogh's painting of the church. It is in violet hues against a sky of deep blue with stained glass windows of ultra-marine.

I walk on to the village centre, to the Auberge Ravoux, still a small restaurant today, and where Van Gogh rented a room. I climb the dark winding staircase to his attic. A skylight is the only source of light.

It was here Van Gogh died. No one has used the room since that day, 29th July 1890. There is nothing to see, just a single chair and bare cracked plaster. But there is something to feel. A great sense of sadness seems trapped within these walls.

Shortly before he died, Van Gogh wrote to his brother about three large canvasses which he had just completed of vast stretches of wheat under stormy skies.

"I didn't have to put myself out very much in order to try and express sadness and extreme loneliness. I'm fairly sure these canvasses will tell you what I cannot say in words, that is how healthy and invigorating I find the countryside."

Sadly, later that month he shot himself in the fields behind the chateau, and, severely wounded, he stumbled back to his room where he died in his brother's arms two days later. He was 37.

Time stands still now in the village of Auvers. It lies within a regional park and according to the charter of the 45 natural parks in France, the village cannot be altered.

In 100 years, it will look as it does today. And today, in many ways, it looks as it did 100 years ago. I hear the clock strike midday. I decide to step back in time and have lunch in the Auberge Ravoux.

Monsieur Bob's Search for his Vines

We call him Monsieur Bob and we follow him along muddy paths and country lanes, trudging through wet grass and woodland. He's clutching sheets of paper with pictures of local landmarks and a list of directions but still he seems strangely disorientated.

He's searching for his vines. Throughout the year his viticulturist tends and prunes and harvests so it is not surprising that Monsieur Bob isn't quite sure where they are. Every row looks the same as the next row, wooden stakes marching in straight lines over hill and valley, like soldiers ready for battle. On and on they sweep making patterns over the land.

It is New Year's Day and the winter landscape of the vineyards of eastern France is bleak and sculptured. No thick green foliage and plump fruit, just bare brown stumps and single shoots, all that is left after winter pruning.

Suddenly he stops. "These are ours," declares Monsieur Bob. We admire his vines. We have drunk copious quantities of his wine over the past few days. It would be churlish not to pay homage to the great providers.

Through a post celebration haze, we gaze at the dark stems and wonder how something so gaunt and beautiful could make us feel so weak and vaguely nauseous. All our New Year vows of abstinence linger unspoken in the recesses of our fuzzy brains.

In Burgundy thousands of acres of vineyards are divided among myriad growers. Sometimes a grower will own just a few rows in a given plot.

We stride on. There is treasure still to find. Another plot, another parcel of vines to locate. Smoke curls up from where a lone viticulturist works, burning the cuttings in his wheelbarrow fire. We hear a woodpecker and watch a buzzard soaring on high.

There can be no better place to discard the old year and embrace the new, an old stone house, surrounded by vines, overlooking the Saône plain. On bright clear days you can see Mont Blanc, 125 miles away, reaching up into the clouds, white and shiny as it catches the rays of the setting sun.

Millions of years ago a hot shallow sea extended to this area from the Jura; a vast emerald lagoon filled with sea creatures, oysters, mussels and scallops. As we walk through the vineyards we find seashells, embedded in the dry-stone walls, hiding under mossy tufts. The vine roots reach down through the ancient seabed grasping nutrients and minerals.

Madame Bob talks of minerality, a contentious term among the wine elite; a belief that minerals from the soil are absorbed by the vines and can be tasted.

And "terroir", the sense of place that imparts its unique quality to the wine.

That evening as we taste another wine, Madame Bob fixes me in her gaze. "Can you taste it," she asks. "Isn't it amazing!" I know she's speaking of that ancient sea. I taste again. "Crushed seashells and a hint of saltiness," I say.

Wine Tasting

Bob nudges me. "Don't ask any more questions," he whispers. "Or we'll never get to taste the wine." He sounds slightly desperate and not surprisingly. We've come, the ten of us, to a wine tasting and an hour later, we still haven't seen a bottle.

We entered by the courtyard door into this pristine, shiny steel fermentation area and the vast tanks which contain the precious liquid stand tall before us.

We are staying in southern Burgundy and Bob has arranged a wine tasting with his friend, viticulturist Christophe. He is clutching a pink hibiscus for Christophe's wife and there are introductions to be made and brave attempts at speaking French. We know the words will flow more easily with the wine later but in the mean time they are stuck somewhere in the back of our brains awaiting lubrication.

Christophe grasps at our ill formed questions and soliloquises. A simple question does not elicit a simple answer. It requires an oration drawing on philosophy, history, geology and so much more.

We edge towards the staircase which leads to the cellar. We feel the cool air rising. Bob is behind me. Then quite involuntarily words slip out about the equipment and how long the tall shiny tanks will last before they need replacing.

Bob tries to silence me with another nudge. Christophe sighs, he looks up, his face contorts and then a torrent of French words pour out, answering my question and so many others I did not find the words to ask.

Finally, we make it to the bottom of the stairs and trudge on soft gravel past row upon row of oak barrels. There are more questions about sourcing the oak and the age of the barrels. There are no short answers. One by one we are learning the cost of our curiosity.

We reach the tasting area. Chairs and stools are provided. The first bottle is produced. The communal sigh is almost audible. The cork is removed. I see Bob relax. Christophe tells us about the year, the conditions, the terroir, the minerality. There is more Shakespearean drama.

And then, only then is the wine poured. I am the first to hold a glass in my hand. Without a thought for poor Bob, I dare to mention 'le changement climatique.'

The bottle is held still. Christophe screws up his eyes, seemingly unsure where to start, the subject so immense. I taste the wine and listen. I am becoming an expert on the effects of climate change on the wine industry. Bob sinks lower onto his stool, staring at the row of empty glasses.

The oration over, more samples are poured and finally Bob holds a glass in his hand. He looks happier now. With each new tasting, French words flow and we become almost as loquacious as our host.

Later as we stumble back to our house, up the steep hill in the dark, past rows of vines, we witness another solo performance - a nightingale trills a rich, joyous song.

Treading the Grapes

Her hands are stained red, the colour of blood. The ruby liquid has seeped under her nails and up round her wrists.

"Every year people die doing this." The young French woman speaks quietly in broken English.

"It is the carbon dioxide from the fermenting grapes. It can kill," she says, her brown eyes shining under dark curling lashes.

She heaves herself along the side of the deep vat and, balancing a rake handle across the top, proceeds to lower herself into the fermenting mass. Her green rubber boots disappear into the bubbling grape mixture. Lifting and lowering herself, using the rake handle and the side of the vat for support, she squelches her boots up and down pushing through the thick morass of skin, stalk and pulp.

This process is 'pigéage'. Twice a day she climbs the metal ladder and balancing precariously along the steel gantry, she clambers on to the side of the vat and proceeds to tread the grapes into the fermenting juice below, a process which helps enrich the flavour and intensity of the wine.

The harvest is over for another year and the lush green slopes of this wine growing region just north west of Macon are beginning the take on the duller hues of autumn. We spend our days, walking and cycling, and of course wine tasting.

But our wine tasting sessions are emotional affairs. I find the wine growers more interesting than the wines themselves. There is Florent who is almost too embarrassed to tell us how his wine had gained the name Pisse Veille. Reluctantly he tells the story. I leave you to guess.

A neighbouring wine grower, Jean, wild curls and gaunt looks, speaks with poetic fervour about his wines. When I ask him which is his favourite he stares and sighs. "I cannot say. My wines are like my children. They are all perfect and I love them all for different reasons."

At another vineyard Robert tells us tales of woe. He speaks of the grêle (hailstones) which damages his grapes and of sickness in the family. He supplements our wine tasting with a feast of paté, bread, bowls of local cheese and wine cake. We do not want the food but we feel obliged to eat. Poor Robert. We cannot turn down this generous feast. We eat, we buy his wine and we eat some more. We even wonder if we should buy a case of wine cake!

We are home now with bottles of wine stowed away in a makeshift cellar. We have yet to put it to the final test. When the cork is pulled will the warmth and pleasure of those wine tasting days emerge with the bouquet. Has it travelled well? We certainly have!

Wedding Champagne

We went in search of champagne for a summer wedding. Not a booze cruise; something far more refined! No trip to a French supermarket to soak up a pool of wine but a planned visit to a proper viticulturist with real vines and magic caves. We wanted to meet the man who made it. We wanted bottles full of bubbles and special memories of a weekend in France with our son and his bride-to-be.

We left shoulder-high cow parsley and flowering elders on the grass verges of England for the tunnel under the sea and the high roads of France, the flat north and the poppy fields of Picardy.

We headed for Epernay at the heart of the Champagne region. We drove along the narrow, undulating road, skirting the little mountain of Reims, through cream and grey villages where every other shuttered house was a *maison de champagne.*

And in the countryside beyond the villages, vineyards stretched in every direction, long tidy rows, green shoots pointing upwards and wavering in the breeze.

We saw a bride on the arm of her father walking through a village to the church. She was holding red roses and smiling and a procession of guests followed in her wake. We were getting in the mood. No long car journey for her to pick up the celebratory nectar.

But we had arrived a day early and Madame wasn't ready. The champagne was still in the cellar. We apologised, our wish to be polite not matched by our disjointed sentences, part French, part English words masquerading as French. I later discovered that *collectionner* does not mean to collect or pick up but to collect for a hobby. No wonder she looked bemused. We had been in the car for three hours and the language switch in our brains was as yet un-oiled.

Then Monsieur appeared. We followed him down a dark, winding staircase to the cellar, the chill in the air increasing with every step. Madame stayed upstairs and started the origami which would turn flat cardboard into champagne boxes with nothing but a twist and turn and sticky tape.

Monsieur was indeed a real viticulturist, stooped and bent like the vines he tended, vineyards that had been in his family for generations. He spoke with passion and his small, intense eyes stared as explanations about his champagne production gushed in rapid French.

Thousands of dusty bottles lay around us. This was where the magic took place. This was where little by little in the silence and cool, the still wine found its bubbles.

We emerged into daylight and loaded the car. Then we were invited inside, into the dining room where Monsieur opened a bottle of unlabelled champagne and served pink biscuits dusted with icing sugar. And we chatted, French words flowing as easily as the champagne and we made the payment, raised a glass to the happy couple and wondered why all costly transactions aren't softened with champagne and pink biscuits.

Italy

For the past 16 years I've skied in the Dolomites in Italy and I've usually found something there to write about. The tale of the missing mountain restaurant was another piece that won the weekly Telegraph travel competition. My favourite is Cows and Dumplings. The stories are all true and so strange that you'd struggle to make them up.

There are two non-skiing tales set in Italy, one about walking the Path of the Gods and the other, a visit to Vesuvius.

Cows and Dumplings

The church clock strikes nine and as if on cue the cloud lifts and we see the sharp edges of the mountain top. The chairlift rises, humming softly in the still morning air. Our black shadow, four stickmen seated on a bar and hanging from a pole, creeps beside us on the snow.

At the top we peel off and make our way down silvery snail pathways, skimming and sliding over the freshly prepared snow. We have a long journey ahead and whisk up and down lifts and slopes to reach the far corners of the Sella Ronda.

We are staying in Canazei in the Dolomites which opens onto Italy's biggest ski carousel with 65 km of ski runs and lifts, set against a backdrop of woods and rocky peaks.

Christmas has long passed but the trumpeting angels still hang from the lamp posts in the town and the chalets shine with coloured lights. But ski resorts have no need of man-made decorations. The snow has its own natural glitter and sparkles like a million diamonds. The bright, white light, renews our spirits after England's grey winter days.

We press on but my skis slip over icy patches and I seem to slither like a snake. We see a sign which tells us there is "few snow" and we dodge round tufts of brown grass.

We reach the wide-open slopes of San Cassiano in the north east corner of the Sella Ronda and sweep down the deserted slopes. Then we start our trek back. We decide to get closer to base before stopping for lunch.

At 2.30 we collapse into a rustic mountain restaurant. We fear that lunch is over. An earnest bespectacled young man ushers us into a pine panelled alcove. He leans over confidentially saying "Yes please lady, what you like?" His English seems good.

My companion apologises for our late arrival and asks: "What time do you finish serving lunch?" The young man stares blankly. "When do you close"? my companion adds, trying to clarify his question. The waiter ponders for a moment and then his face lights up as if with great comprehension and he smiles: "Ah yes," he says. "We have lovely dumplings."

On our homeward journey we venture down a black run and are overtaken by a young man clad only in black underpants and red ski boots. The temperature is minus 5. He skis quickly. I shudder as I watch him pass.

The day ends even more bizarrely. We take the cable car down to the village. For company we have three young German men dressed as Friesian cows. A black furry bull sits in the corner. I discuss with my companion my lack of control on icy patches and I'm unsure whether to blame my technique or my skis.

Speaking English with a strong German accent, the cow on my left informs me: "The edges of your skis should be sharp enough to cut down fir trees. If not, you should get them sharpened." I am mesmerized by the four pink plastic udders on his stomach which quiver as he speaks. I look round the cable car and the other cows agree. The bull in the corner nods. I haven't taken bovine advice before but I think, on this occasion, I will.

The Hidden Valley

She wanted to go to the Hidden Valley and she wouldn't take 'no' for an answer. We sat around the table in the Tyrolean restaurant, weary from a morning's skiing, sipping coffee and a strange, bright orange, medicinal tasting wine from thin glass goblets.

Her round pearl earrings, the size of mint imperials, waggled as she nodded emphatically, insisting that we were so close, we just had to go there. We, the seven others in the ski group, were not convinced. One person had been there several years earlier, but couldn't remember the way. We only knew that it was not a journey to be undertaken on a whim. It needed a bit of planning, an early start and at some stage, a bus or taxi and horses. There was a clue to its accessibility, or lack of it, in the name.

But Linda, Italian in all but name and birth, was not put off. She prodded the ski map vigorously, pointing to the lifts and runs required to discover this hidden place. We had skied with her for four days and she had proved to be delightful but assertive, reprimanding anyone who skied too close to her, waving her arms and gesticulating wildly.

We were near Corvara in the Italian Dolomites where heavy snow falls had provided perfect skiing conditions. The white gloved fingers of the pine trees pointed to the frozen ground and lace makers had been at work on the delicate branches of the larch trees.

We had heard a lot about the Hidden Valley with its spectacular frozen waterfalls and ski run that twisted and turned to the valley bottom where a pair of horses would drag skiers over the frozen river bed to the next lift. During the First World War this was the front between the Italian and Austro-Hungarian forces. There was also a war museum to visit. Our battle was strictly verbal.

Linda had joined our group declaring she did not know the area and wanted some help to find her way around. She sat silently for a few moments, studying the map, sipping her fluorescent medication. Then she turned to the waiter, showing him the map and asking for directions. He patiently pointed the way, describing in detail the lifts and runs. She thanked him and, turning triumphantly towards us, declared: "Two hours. It will only take two hours. We can do it." She smiled and her shiny white teeth matched her shiny white ski jacket.

We stared vacantly, overcome with a certain languor, an overwhelming feeling of idleness. We had skied many miles over several days. It was almost midday now. A lingering lunch in a mountain restaurant beckoned enticingly.

Then, quite without prompting, one of the women in the group spoke and with genuine sincerity, summed up our feelings. "Thank you, Linda, for putting so much effort into organising something none of us wants to do."

It seemed that the Hidden Valley would remain hidden for some time to come.

The Missing Restaurant

Snow can play tricks on the mind. All that white stuff can cause hallucinations. So, I did not take too seriously my husband's suggestion that the restaurant where we'd intended to have lunch had literally disappeared.

"It's gone!" he exclaimed. "I don't understand. It was there last year. Do you remember? You do remember, don't you?"

It's fair to say I did remember having lunch somewhere in the area but I am not known for my map-reading skills. Working out a piste map is like a game of snakes and ladders without the dice. Put me in the mountains among those tall white peaks and I become topographically disorientated.

So, in the end, we had only his word that the restaurant had actually been on the particular slope we were now drifting past in the lift

He turned and looked back down the slope, craning his neck around as the lift eased us gently towards the summit.

"Ah but there is a restaurant on the other side of the piste." He sounded relieved. "They must have moved the piste."

127

I glanced back. I sighed. "Not unless they also planted a copse of mature pine trees and moved those massive rocks." I may not be an orienteering master but I can spot an engineering and horticultural impossibility.

We had brought a group of skiers from Canazei in the Italian Dolomites to have lunch in the non-existent restaurant. We had skied for miles around the Sella Ronda and turned off towards Ortisei.

We had taken the train through the mountain, pinned together with strangers, shoulders, backs, stomachs touching, no personal space; warm breath in our faces. Maybe he was suffering from oxygen deprivation, I wondered.

As we edged upwards, he continued to stare down the slope in disbelief. I continued to enjoy the view.

In this landscape, where snowy slopes were patterned with great swirls and pine cones hung like sausages from trees, there was so much more to take my attention than a missing mountain restaurant.

A flock of choughs circled above us as we emerged from the lift and started to ski down. After several minutes we arrived at the place where the restaurant used to be. And there was indeed a gap. However, on the other side of the slope was another restaurant.

"We might as well try this one," my husband said disconsolately.

We sat down and the waiter arrived. My husband could not resist asking.

"Whatever happened to the restaurant on the other side of the piste?"

"You're in it," was the reply.

"I told you. They moved the piste," he said triumphantly.

"No, we moved the restaurant. Took it down plank by plank and rebuilt it here. It's a better position."

I could see the glazed look of relief on my husband's face. Not a case of snow-induced hallucination after all.

"Phew," was all I could say.

The Long March

From my hotel window they looked like giant stick insects, quite angular and spindly, as they swarmed along the snowy path. But as they approached, I could see them bowing and bobbing and their movements seemed smooth and rhythmical; hundreds of them marching through the valley.

I left the hotel and skittered down to the track to watch. A group of hotel staff had already gathered. This was no insect procession. These were elite athletes, sleek, Lycra clad men and women, jaws set, thighs hard as steel, skis long and thin, and turned up at the ends like elves' shoes. I heard a clicking like metal knitting needles as the first group approached and their ski sticks hit the snow.

The Marcialonga, a 70km race through the Valleys of Fiemme and Fassa in the Dolomites, is one Italy's most challenging endurance cross-country skiing races and attracts eight thousand competitors from all over the world.

The cow bell clanged as Luciano, the hotel owner, approached and we cheered and shouted in support. Race veteran, Luciano a competitor for 40 years, managed a smile; there was no sign of exertion, no heavy breathing, just power and passion.

We'd been in the area for a week, downhill skiing. We felt we'd undergone a bit of an endurance test ourselves but as we watched the cross-country skiing, we realised we were mere wimps by comparison. This race took strength and fitness to another level.

High in the mountains the pistes were well covered with snow but here in the valley, in the balmy unseasonal air, the snow had diminished daily and the grass, brown and knotted, had pushed through. Race organisers moved more than 40,000 lorry loads of snow and deposited it along the track to ensure the Marcialonga could take place.

Once our veteran hero had sped past, we left by coach to drive to Venice for our flight home. We followed the race along the valley. And still they kept coming, an endless stream of Lowry folk, bent like old men, their posture belying their fitness as they slid and skimmed over the snow, flashes of blue, orange and red against the black pines, a helicopter buzzing overhead.

At one point we caught a glimpse of the track on the far side of the river, where the elite competitors were already gliding along the home straight, while on the path closest to us, the slower ones, less lean, more chunky, their body shape in keeping with their position in the race, plodded on. Some could have been taking a Sunday afternoon stroll.

When at last we swept into the mountain tunnel at Moena and the race disappeared from view, a friend turned to me and sighed: "I feel quite exhausted after watching all that exertion."

"Time for a power nap then," I suggested.

"No", he said, yawning. I need something longer and more relaxing."

Sunrise in the Dolomites

I waited patiently on the frozen mountain top. Even though the temperature was minus 17 and my face and fingers seemed to have become detached from my body, I stood firm.

The birds were waiting too. A flock of Alpine choughs circled and danced in anticipation. They were limbering up for the new day, spinning and twirling.

I had limbered up. Well lumbered up really. I had joined a slow progression of people, traipsing up the steep slope. Ski boots, rigid and skiddy, were never meant for walking but I'd plodded on in calf deep snow, tripping and falling and crouching, to ease my way up.

Some found the climb easier than others. A young woman, nimble footed like a mountain goat, whisked past me, well balanced and steady, a fine glass of champagne clutched in her thick gloved hand. She was ready to celebrate. It was all I could do to hang on and stop myself slithering back down the slope.

I was spending a week skiing in the Dolomites of northern Italy. It was Louise's idea to leave warm beds at 5am. She fixed me with her wide, blue eyes. "Surely you want to see the pink glow as the sun rises over the snowy mountains." What is it about sunrise on holiday that makes people do foolish things?

I'd got up, travelled by taxi on a deserted road to the bottom of the mountain and entered the plastic cocoon of the bubble lift which purred its way up through the dark, frozen landscape. At the top the silence was broken by the slap of skis on hard snow, the click of boots into bindings and a sound of crushing ice as our skis cut into corduroy snow with only moonbeams to light our way.

A chair-lift zipped us up still higher, across the grey land. We drank sweet tea ladled from a cauldron over burning logs and then started our slow climb to the highest point.

The black birds were still circling above. We stamped our feet and swung our arms. The young woman stared into her glass in dismay as ice crystals formed and froze the champagne.

In the east, sharp black mountain teeth cut the sky. Gradually the darkness dispersed and strangely the western range lit up in fifty shades of pink. But there was still no sign of the sun in the east. We would surely freeze to death before we'd feel its warmth. Time to go.

We trundled down the path, the young woman even swifter now that her champagne was in no danger of spilling. We put on skis and with the moon a mere white smudge in the brightening sky, we snaked and turned and forced the blood back into our fingers and toes. We took another chair lift and sat scanning the eastern sky. Finally, the sun appeared, sparkling like a precious diamond and turned the white land into a glittering paradise.

A Cake Decorator's Dream

Spring skiing can take you to a cake decorator's paradise. Royal icing, fluffy frosting and butter cream all feature on the snowy pistes of Italy during the balmy days of spring.

I am skiing with a group in Pozza di Fassa and it is there, in late March that I ski in my own fantasy world, changing from skier to sugarcrafter as the mood takes me.

I awake on the first day and the landscape has been transformed, flattened overnight by huge palette knives, patting and smoothing the ruffled snow. I step out onto iced cookies, hard crunchy lumps. My skis merely sweep over the surface. I desperately try to cut in and control my movement but the surface stays rigid, the cookies stay intact, more of a nut crunch, shatter proof and unbreakable.

I glide through the magic kingdom of a run called Citta dei Sassi – City of Rocks, but for me it is a city of Christmas cakes, gentle domed rocks, covered in royal icing and each topped with a small Christmas tree. Above me tower the giant iced muffins, the snowy mountains of the Sella Ronda. Away from the piste, where the snow has melted, the marzipan grass has not yet been coloured green.

By mid-morning I am chasing, racing and dashing over icing sugar, glace icing, pure white and shiny with the squeaky sound of fresh snow. It is soft but firm and my skis carve and shape it. I glide through it in gentle swirling movements. I am sculpting the landscape, making mounds of iced fancies, fairy cakes and cupcakes topped with delicious icing.

The sun comes out and the baking starts. The icing sugar turns to caster sugar and I can use it for mixing and blending, my skis working like food processor blades, whisking and churning.

After a break for lunch the raw materials of my cake making dream have become heavy. The hot sun has turned the snow into thick granulated sugar and someone must have added some syrup because it is now gluey and my skis falter and stick. I fight my way through it, pushing and kneading. There are patches of Demerara and Barbados sugar, dark brown and moist. It adds colour and flavour to my cakes but plays havoc with my skiing.

I take a chairlift to higher slopes. I can see the shining meringues in the distance, lit by the late afternoon sun, polished and brushed with silver glitter. Like all good meringues they are crisp on the outside and mouth wateringly soft on the inside. In the distance the marshmallow fields are lightly dusted with powder.

Exhilarated and exhausted, my sugarcrafting is over for another day. I pray that the overnight frost will not be too heavy and that in the morning the snow will not be quite so hard. Perhaps someone will add a drop of glycerine. I use it when I'm baking. It helps to keep the icing soft.

A Big Muddy Hole

I waited on a corner of the narrow incline to take breath. A woman trudged down the slope towards me, stopped and held on to a wooden post.

"It gets really steep at the top," she said. "And when you get there it's just a big muddy hole. It's not worth the effort."

Her husband came alongside, panting. "I didn't make it. I didn't see it," he said.

I muttered consolatory words, smiled and carried on up the path. My feet were being sucked into the loose earth. There were posts on one side of the path and, strung between them, a thick rope, to shield walkers from the almost vertical drop. But in places, the posts had just disappeared in a slide of loose mud. Scrubby pines and bushes clung to the slope and provided some stability. I kept close to the inside edge, at times a wall of rock and at others, consolidated mud. It seemed safer. I climbed higher. I took my time.

A minicab had dropped me further down the mountain at the part where the road ended and the track began. We had woven round narrow roads past small hotels and umbrella pines, vineyards and lemon groves and then just rocky outcrops and sparse vegetation. "I'll wait for 90 minutes," the driver had said, as we spilled out of the cab.

I was getting tired now. I thought about the woman's comments. Would it be worth the climb, I wondered. The sun blazed down and my boots filled with grit.

Finally, I reached the top. A lizard balanced precariously on the rim. I peered down. Not just a big muddy hole after all but an arid cauldron of immense proportions; no fire, no smoke but a 650-foot slide into hell. This was the inside of the mighty volcano, Vesuvius, which had wiped out Pompeii and Herculaneum. It now lay sleeping in the afternoon sun.

I continued to walk around the edge, staring down into the great hollow, imagining the fire and fury that had sprung from its depths. Earlier in the day I'd seen the devastation it had caused far below; the wall of mud and lava that had poured into Herculaneum and the hot ash and cinders that had showered down on the people of Pompeii. I'd seen the long grey river of lava, solid on the slopes where it last spewed out its anger just 70 years earlier.

After I had inspected the big muddy hole and, with my mind full of the horrors of the eruption and the latent power of the mighty volcano, I trudged back down the track. The driver was waiting patiently. I climbed into the cab.

As I looked down over Naples I wondered about the next eruption. Was there an evacuation plan in place to avoid a repeat of the 79AD massacre? But what would happen if the great beast stirred and started rumbling now?

I need not have worried. My driver proved he could drive faster than any lava flow. He was obviously already in training. I hung on and held my breath.

Path of the Gods

Nino, our walking guide, promised to take us to the best restaurant in Italy for lunch but how he would manage to combine fine dining with a remote mountain walk, I wasn't sure.

We were to walk the Path of the Gods, a high and heavenly way above the Amalfi Coast in Italy, a path still used today by farmers to transport their produce across this wild and precipitous terrain.

We took the local train to Castellammare and then a bus which wound up mountain roads past lemon groves and olive trees and meadows of bright yellow flowers. As we crossed the top of the peninsula, we caught a glimpse of the sea on both sides.

At Bomerano, the small village where the Path of the Gods begins, we stopped for coffee in a small family run café and Nino chatted with the owners, Italian words spilling into one another. We admired, but resisted, the St Josephs' Day cakes in the large glass cabinet, big iced balls, like profiteroles full of cream with soft icing and a cherry on the top.

Then we set off in thick mist down stone steps out of the village. We knew the sea was somewhere below us but we couldn't see it. It was actually 1800 feet down and in places the rocky drop was almost vertical.

The path is an ancient track high above the Mediterranean. For centuries it was the only route for local people and travellers. Farmers still work the narrow terraces, little plots balanced on the hillside. A man who was planting potatoes greeted us as we emerged from the mist. We could hear, but not see, the goats whose bells clanged high in the mountain.

Nino stopped to point out wild violets growing in rocky crevices and he picked a tiny white flower so we could smell its honey scent. There was mint and wild thyme and high bushes of white heather. Then, as if we had stepped into the past, a man on a mule came towards us; the mule picking its way carefully over the rocky ground.

The mist cleared a little and we looked down on the village of Priano which seemed to grow out of the mountainside, and the Convent of St Domenica with its neatly tilled terraces and vineyards. At times Nino strode ahead, nimbly picking his way like the mule we had seen. At other times he walked with us, pointing out emerald euphorbia and lapillo, a white, light volcanic rock.

At midday we rounded a rocky corner. Nino had found a picnic bench on a precipice and he'd laid out a crusty loaf, sweet tomatoes, fat olives and a local cheese, caciocavallo, which looked like a giant pear.

As we sat down, the mist lifted, the sun came out and the sea shone like tinsel. The bells in the church tower in the village below chimed midday and the sound echoed round the mountain. Bees buzzed in the purple rosemary. It was, without doubt, the best restaurant in Italy.

Sri Lanka

This jewel in the Indian Ocean provided me with enough material for a book on its own but I have restricted myself to five tales. They sum up an amazing country and give a taste of everyday life there.

We were lucky enough to be touring with a great group of people and our new found friend, Bernie, kept us amused for much of the trip.

Elephant Procession

The traffic jam started on the outskirts of Pussellawa, Sri Lanka. Lorries, buses, cars and tuk tuks were jammed on both sides of the road. There seemed no way to go. But with a bicycle there's always a small gap to squeeze through.

We swerved in and out of the traffic, broke every cycling rule. We pushed and shoved our way round people and cars and squashed ourselves between high sided lorries and buses, belching black fumes.

And there in front of us was an elephant, a huge pink elephant. We'd cycled long and hard, up bend after bend; the heat was oppressive. Pools of water prickled our skin. We felt a little feverish so we would not have been surprised to see pink elephants. This one was real.

We heard a beating of drums, blasting of trumpets and shrill whistles. A policeman waved his arms and urged us to move our bikes off the road. The elephant, resplendent in pink and red jewelled overcoat and headdress, lead a procession of women in purple and pink silk saris; there were ripples of colour, splashes of orange and red. The women walked behind the elephant pulling a wheeled temple, children in tall orange headdresses followed and then the men, muscular bare-chested men, wearing white sarongs.

It was an extraordinary, chaotic scene, a mutli-coloured microcosm of Sri Lankan life on the streets of a small town. As the procession passed and we cycled on out of town, we passed a funeral cortege, a black car bedecked with flowers. Men and women dressed in black and white were walking up the hill. We skittered past, embarrassed, uncomfortable, intrusive spectators at another aspect of local life.

But this was the real pleasure of cycling in Sri Lanka. We could have gone by car but we wanted to see everything close-to and experience the sights, sounds and smells of the country. We wanted to see behind the tourist veneer and take the roads less travelled.

Our cycling took us along river banks, canals, lakeside paths, and undulating rural back roads. At every turn of the pedal, every bend in the road, we felt the thrill of the unexpected. We saw huge, muddy elephant footprints on the tarmac, glimpsed the flash of the white throated kingfisher, watched monkeys tightrope walking on the wires across the road, saw close to the green pimples on the giant jackfruit on roadside stalls, smelled the wood burning fires and eyeballed the crocodiles in the lakes

Every day was full of surprises and strange and beautiful moments. It wasn't just the unusual things we noticed. We saw the commonplace; the stray dogs, hundreds of them, and the smiles on the faces of the children who raced to their front gates to wave and shout friendly greetings. We witnessed the gentle rhythm of everyday life.

One evening we headed down an orange, dusty road to a village in the Tambalawawe district to a family living in a simple home in the jungle. The man, an agricultural worker, told us that he had been bitten 21 times by snakes.

The man's wife prepared a traditional vegetarian meal of rice, dahl and bean curry with spicy greens and coconut and cooked it over a fire in the garden where only the previous week they had discovered elephant footprints quite close to the house. We sat at a long wooden table under a teak tree and the moon shone down and lightning flashed across the sky.

Hindu Blessing

It seemed a good idea to receive a Hindu blessing at the start of my 445 km cycling holiday in Sri Lanka. At 71, I needed all the help I could get.

Anything that would save me from elephant stampedes, big hairy spiders lurking behind toilet doors, and local buses, built like tanks and travelling at the speed of sound, would be worthwhile.

I had taken off my shoes at the entrance to the sacred Buddhist cave temples at Dambulla. My feet were burning on the hot stone slabs. I was anxious to reach the cool interior of the cave. The holy man was seated at a table by the door. I stopped and bowed my head and he tied a piece of string around my wrist and he chanted special words, and money changed hands.

A fellow cyclist followed. I noticed that she paid him more money and she seemed to receive a longer blessing but maybe these were just my unholy thoughts.

It was my first day on this exotic island. We had cycled all morning through quiet back roads and forest; we'd passed rice fields edged with slender trunked palm trees, balsa trees and teak trees with leaves the size of tennis rackets.

The cycling was easy; the road surface was better than at home. But it was hot. Sri Lanka was in the throes of a heatwave and I had my very own reservoir concealed under my cycling helmet. Every now and then a stream would trickle down my face.

We watched children playing in the river and we also found a stream, well away from the crocodiles, to cool ourselves down. Still in cycling clothes we waded into the gushing water and clung on to rocks to avoid being swept downstream.

Later we headed into the Hill Country. I'd survived the heat but would I survive the hills? We started our climb up towards the tea plantations. We pedalled slowly, bend after bend, cocks crowing, jackfruit the size of rugby balls hanging from the trees, pink bananas and giant water melons on roadside stalls.

Up and up we went and the vegetation changed. There were leggy eucalyptus and cypress trees and the air was fresher with aromas of pine and wild mint. We could see the sturdy tea bushes, closely planted in ridges like well-trimmed hedges.

After nearly four hours of pedalling, I gave up. I got off my bike and walked the last 300 yards to the tea plantation.

But, of course the struggle to cycle uphill had its reward. The next day we free-wheeled downhill for two and a half hours.

We'd managed the most testing part of the trip. Now we enjoyed a few days of gently undulating terrain in the south west of the country and a final day by the Indian Ocean.

We'd kept our string bracelets on all holiday. They changed from pure white to the colour of the soil. We'd escaped snake bites, rabid dogs and elephant tramplings. And it didn't seem to matter how much we gave the holy man we all survived the fortnight unscathed.

The Waiting Game

They play a waiting game in the still waters of the Udawalawe reservoir in Sri Lanka; it's like musical statues at a children's party. No creature moves.

Hundreds of dead trees, waist deep in water, stand like stone sculptures, stark and beautiful in the eerie landscape.

On the high branches, the eagle casts a watchful eye. Lower down cormorants and Indian herons rest, and in the water, egrets and terns, painted storks and pelicans pose. A sandpiper balances on one yellow leg.

They are watching for the next morsel, not daring to move in case they become that morsel. The silence is unnerving. Water buffalo, shiny black boulders, horns like sticks, lie with nostrils resting just above the surface of the water. And just beneath the surface with only glassy eyes and a patch of leathery skin visible, lie the crocodiles.

We are the first to make a move. The engine of our safari jeep revs up and the game resumes. There's a wild flapping of wings, white sails in the air. The water buffalo shift their great bulk. A ripple of water crinkles round the crocodiles. A pelican scoots across the path.

The enormous Udawalawe Reservoir is a wildlife haven. It was built in 1963 to irrigate agricultural areas nearby and also to generate electricity. The dead trees standing in the water are a reminder of the extent of the forest cover before the construction of the dam

The Udawalawe National Park was created nine years later to protect the area around the reservoir. The park is best known for its large resident population of elephants, believed to number about 600.

We are on a cycling holiday in Sri Lanka taking the back roads, seeing the country and its people close-to. For the safari trip we abandoned our bikes for the safety of a jeep.

But now we're back in the saddle pedalling our way through quiet roads and alongside canals and lakes. We swelter in 34 degrees. I hallucinate about the ice hotel in Lapland and I stare longingly at great expanses of cool water.

And there are plenty. Sri Lanka's irrigation system is impressive. The island's Sinhalese people produced skilled hydraulic engineers who built some of the largest manmade irrigation works in the world. There are thousands of reservoirs from small village ponds to vast lakes and an intricate network of canals which supply water to acres of paddy fields and to towns and villages.

Our final days in this exotic island are spent by the ocean at Unawatuna, near the southerly tip. We watch the surf breaking on the sandy beach and stare out at the great expanse of blue water and take a moment to ponder the wise words of the great 12th century King Parakramabahu: "Not even a drop of water that comes from rain should flow into the ocean without being made useful to man." His words are still relevant today.

Looking for Leopards

"I do believe I told Sam it was going to rain," Bernadette declared.

The safari jeep jolted over tracks of orange earth, deeper and deeper into the Yala National Park in Sri Lanka. We watched the black clouds gathering. A laser beam of lightning sliced the sky and the thunder burst. Then the rain cascaded down and the earth turned red and the gullies filled with water.

"What did he say?" I asked.

"He just said the forecast's not accurate," Bernadette's soft Irish tone and mocking smile revealing more than her words.

We were looking for leopards and sloth bears, and elephants, if there were any, but we'd seen so many the previous day that we felt quite relaxed on the elephant front. Leopards? That was another matter entirely.

We stopped for a while gazing into the distance at a crack in the rock where Sam, our tour leader, said a leopard was lying. I could only see granite and greenery.

"It's just a few spots. It hasn't even got a face. For all we know someone could have thrown down an old coat," Bernadette declared.

As we moved on, the rain eased. But we were soaked and were beginning to lose interest in leopard sightings. Suddenly the jeep took off. Someone had reported leopards nearby. Everyone else had heard too. More than twenty jeeps converged at a crossroads, all jostling for the best viewing position.

We could see the leopards clearly; two young males were lounging on the long branch of a rain tree. A leopard sighting is rare in the park and a double sighting rarer still.

But there was an even rarer occurrence – a jungle traffic jam. The jam became more entertaining than the leopards. People were taking photographs of the trucks pushing and shoving and manoeuvring just inches apart. Our driver managed to squeeze through the melee and we were on our way.

Big muddy puddles lay deep and still on the track ahead. It was impossible to know how deep they were until the jeep hit them. On a particularly rutted stretch the jeep sunk, the driver revved the engine, the mud sprayed up and the wheels whizzed round, digging deeper and deeper into the earth.

The truck began to list like a sinking boat. It was almost on its side when we were told to 'abandon jeep'. Now we stood well away from the jeep in the scrubby bush among the yellow flowering ranawara and the last thing we wanted to see was a leopard or an elephant.

We waited, glancing round nervously, while the driver struggled to free the truck. Eventually it lurched forward and we scrambled back in. "It was worth it," Bernadette said. "Two leopards in a tree and one in a rock."

"The record is seven leopards at a water hole," Sam said.

"It's better to see two in a tree and one in a rock than hear about seven at a water hole," Bernadette replied.

It all sounded to me a bit like the old proverb about birds, hands and bushes.

Incident at Lion Rock

It became known as the incident at Lion Rock. And like all Irish tales it grew spectacularly as the days went by. In the end we almost believed that Bernadette had jumped 620 feet from the rock, and survived.

We were climbing to the top of the rocky outcrop of Sigiriya in the central Matale district of Sri Lanka to see the ruins of a 5th century palace-fortress.

We'd started early. Sam, our guide, had an unnatural fear of being caught in crowds. We had to get there in good time or we'd be stuck on the ascent. We had 40 km to cycle later in the day to reach our next hotel.

We strode through the palace gardens, past moats and water gardens, the great Lion Rock, stark and square loomed above us.

We were in the shady west approach. The heat was already intense. It was like walking in a fan assisted oven. The climb would be hard, 1,200 steps. We started up the solid stone stairway cut in the rock.

We stopped half-way and mounted a spiral staircase to a sheltered gallery in the sheer rock face to see the famous damsel frescoes, more than 2,000 years old, bare-breasted women, still in the full flush of youth as if painted yesterday. We continued the climb.

Bernadette and I took our time, gasping on ledges. Sam looked anxiously back. He could see the crowds coming. Crocodiles of school children dressed in white, snaked along the path.

We reached the terrace with the lion's claws, great pads of stone at the foot of the final metal gantry. We had emerged from the shade and were now in full sun. Moisture trickled down onto my lip. My hair stuck to my head. I glanced at Bernadette. Her cheeks were flushed.

We stumbled on. One thousand one hundred and ninety nine, one thousand two hundred. And then we were at the top. We'd reached the ruins of the ancient palace, the four-acre summit with spectacular views over jungle and forest. Bernadette stepped quickly across the gritty surface and climbed onto a large boulder.

"One thousand, two hundred and one," she declared. "Are you ready Sam?" She handed over her camera.

"Jump", he said. "I'll get you in mid-air."

Bernadette jumped and for a second she flew through the air and then fell all of nine inches, hitting the ground with a dull thud like a stone. She was sprawled across the pink gravel, blood spurting from both knees. Sam had captured her short flight on camera. He then spent the next 20 minutes stemming the flow of blood and patching up her injured knees.

Later in the week I heard Bernadette talking to the driver of our minibus. In soft Irish tones and with a sardonic smile, she enquired: "Did Sam tell you I jumped off Lion Rock?"

"Yes," he said. "And you survived!"

"Just a few cuts," she said. The story was gathering dramatic effect.

Malaysia, Thailand, Cambodia and Vietnam

We travelled by train in Malaysia but the Thailand, Cambodia and Vietnam trip was another cycling holiday.

There were many sad tales and much of what we saw and heard was quite grim, particularly in Cambodia.

Sharm's story illustrates only too well what the people of Cambodia have suffered in the past.

There were many thought-provoking moments in Vietnam too and to see the tunnel life of the Viet Cong was chilling.

A Breath of Sea Air

The bus is late. Not just a few minutes but an hour. We have travelled north by jungle train up the Malaysian peninsula to Kota Bharu so we are aware of the vagaries of the transport system. But it is hot and we are weary.

We are waiting in the busy terminal where buses pant and gasp like thirsty animals but ours does not come. An old woman selling nuts takes pity on us and offers us shade under her umbrella.

"Where you go?" she asks, her dark eyes staring through black-rimmed glasses beneath a black Islamic scarf.

"To the beach. We want some sea air", we reply.

"You want number 9 bus? Wait here. You sit?" She offers us a once white plastic chair now grey with grime.

I want to ask her what she is selling but fear she might encourage us to try some. It would be rude to refuse. I recognise the monkey nuts but there are other strange products. Some are small and dark like tiny furry creatures and others look like mud encrusted new potatoes.

It's 3pm and the schools have closed. Young Muslim girls in pure white hijab and long lavender skirts swarm into the terminal, laughing and chattering and carrying piles of books.

A vagrant with a two-foot-long mane of matted hair slopes across the road towards us. He is making for a rubbish bin. He sorts through the debris and retrieves a half-drunk carton of red juice. He sucks up the remains through the used straw.

An ancient Chinese man wearing a sarong, Chinese hat and carrying a silver topped cane shuffles across the road. He looks as though he has slipped out of a scene on my mother's Chinese vase.

The sweat is now dripping from my brow. We go back to the ticket office.

"The bus still hasn't come," we say.

"Go and ask over there." He points to a small kiosk we had not seen on the far side of the bus terminal. We venture over.

"When is the number 9 bus coming?"

"Soon," the man replies and then after a moment of reflection he adds: "Maybe".

We abandon the idea of a bus and decide to take a taxi. We find the drivers at the far end of the rank clustered round an open bonnet.

"How much would it cost to go to the beach?"

"Which beach you want?"

We produce a map which they examine.

"How long will it take to get there?"

"Half an hour but the traffic is very bad. An hour, maybe more. Longer to get back, busy time."

A simple trip has turned into an epic journey. "We won't go," we say. They look relieved. A swim in

the hotel pool beckons invitingly.

The Border Crossing

"Beware of everyone and stay together," Buhn, our guide tells us. We are leaving Thailand and driving to the Poipet International border to enter Cambodia.

"There will be good people and bad people, people hanging around from the casinos, desperate people travelling from one side to the other, villagers and traders, children trying to trick you and pick pockets," he says. The list seems endless.

We have to leave our coach at the border and go on foot. It is mayhem. People are going in every direction, there are hundreds of motor scooters, nearly all with masked riders; there are trucks and a few cars. Everyone looks grim and intent on their purpose. Thousands of people cross the border every day for work and gambling and the noise of traffic is a great roar in our ears and everywhere is a smell of fumes and stale fish. The paving is cracked and rough. We cross a metal gantry and then the Friendship Bridge which was built by the British and is looking distinctly unfriendly.

We enter a small office and join one of four lines of people queuing towards a wide counter with a metal grill. On my right is a small shrine and a brass urn.

A large sign tells us we should have no weapons, cameras, videos or cell phones. Another says there is nothing to pay. Another, please stand behind the line. The room is silent.

We stand behind the line and wait. And wait. When we eventually reach the counter, we are told we need to fill in another visa entry form. We've already filled in one but that was taken at the first check point.

We move to one side and fill in forms, then try to mingle in at the front of the queue. After all we'd made it to the front once. We didn't want to start again. A tiny woman becomes agitated. She huffs and tuts and then starts pushing people out of the way. We let her go in front rather than risk an international incident.

Tracy, a Canadian in our party, reaches the grill and is asked for fingerprints. She places her four fingers flat on the screen as directed and waits. Eventually the official grunts and signifies she should lift her hand. He then gives her a thumbs-up sign. Tracy is so delighted that the whole intimidating procedure is over that she returns the thumbs-up sign, lifting both thumbs and smiling broadly with relief. She is met with a severe frown and a shaking of both thumbs by the official. His is not a thumbs-up sign of approval. He isn't happy. He wants her thumb prints.

We make it through the border and our next coach is waiting at the other side. We sit on purple and gold seats, with purple tasselled pelmets at the window. We meet our new guide Sharm and he passes the journey telling tales of Cambodia under the evil Khmer Rouge. We watch the tassels on the purple pelmets wavering in the breeze and feel justifiably uneasy about our recent border crossing.

Sharm's Story

He smiles a lot, a wide smile, straight teeth. He laughs a lot too. Too much for some in our tour party.

It takes only a few days for us to realise that the smile conceals a great sadness. Sharm, our Cambodian tourist guide, was a child at the time of the Khmer Rouge and the campaign to deprive the country of its culture and civilisation and fill the soil with a mountain of bones and a sea of blood.

Sharm takes us to the Tuoi Sleng Genocide Museum. It used to be a school until it became a torture and interrogation centre. We see the yellow walls, yellow and white tiled floor, a bed with manacles attached for daily torture. The walls are full of victims' photographs. They are staring at us.

"That could have been me," Sharm says, pointing to a black and white picture of young boys carrying soil in bags, held from canes over sagging shoulders, bodies bowing under the strain. The boys are skinny, weak and with a frightened look in their eyes. They are moving soil to build dams.

Sharm tells us his story. He was taken from his family when he was 10 to help build dams. He lived away from home for two years. He ate geckos and rats, anything to fill his belly. He became so homesick that he escaped. He left at night and walked along the river bank but barking dogs gave away his position and Khmer Rouge soldiers chased him and fired at him and he hid in the rice fields.

Eventually he made it home and his mum and dad hugged him and gave him food and his mother sat up all night, fanning him to keep him cool and keep away the mosquitos. The following night his father woke him in the early hours and told him he must return to the camp or his family would be killed. "You are a man now," he said.

His father took him to the river and built a raft out of banana canes. "I was so frightened," Sharm says. He made it back to the camp and hid, and then lined up with the other boys when the bell rang.

Sharm takes us to the Killing Fields of Choeung Ek where the bodies of 17,000 people were found, one of thousands of such sites. There are grassy hollows now where the bones were unearthed. We see a jaw bone and teeth which have washed to the surface amid the roots of a palm tree. We see the killing tree where babies were swung and battered and the grave where the bodies of one hundred women and children were found.

We see a glass tower filled with human skulls. We are numb with the evil of war. As we walk away a cock crows. There is a strange stillness in the air. Sharm is waiting for us. He isn't smiling now. His face is smudged with tears.

The Fall and Rise of a Cyclist

Darren didn't smile much on our cycling trip, even before he fell off his bike – three times.

We were cycling from Bangkok to Saigon and the terrain, whilst not difficult, was a little tricky. Tricky for a man used to a road bike. Darren found chubby tyres not completely to his liking.

His first tumble came on a gritty road in Thailand. He caught the wheel of the bike in front and hit the ground heavily. His hand and wrist went black, bruised not broken. The second time was in Cambodia. He came round a corner and collided with another member of our group and actually landed on top of her, thus breaking his fall, but he still managed to injure his wrist. The other one.

On our last cycling day, we left our homestay on an island in the Mekong Delta and sped round narrow tracks, some paved, some gritty, through waterside villages. The challenging parts were the little concrete bridges spanning canals and irrigation channels. They rose steeply, were only just over a metre wide and had no sides. You had to focus on where you wanted to go, rather than where you didn't want to end up. You had to make sure you were in the right gear and hope and pray you didn't meet a motor scooter on the brow coming in the opposite direction.

Darren fell off as he descended one, and ended up in wet mud, hurting both wrists and cutting his knees and back. "You'll be alright now. You've had three falls," his friends said, reassuringly. After that they tried to keep him away from hazards – electric weaving looms, busy roads and machetes used to cut sweets.

On the last day we visited the tunnels used by the Viet Cong to outwit the US military in the Vietnam War. We saw traps that turned and twisted, rolled and folded. There were fish traps and seesaws, all with sharpened barbs or spikes to mutilate their prey. We saw booby traps which lay beneath leafy forest floors. We saw how inventive the evil of war can be. The underground world of weapons, hidden hospitals, kitchens where they cooked with no smoke and sandals which left backward facing footsteps.

We peered into the warren of underground tunnels. They were so low and narrow that few of us were prepared to step down, to fold our bodies and crawl into the confined spaces. One or two braved the shortest passage of just 20 metres. Darren opted for the 100-metre stretch.

We waited anxiously on the surface, not knowing where or if ever he would come to the surface. "We shouldn't have let him go. Not with his record," his concerned friends joked. We could hear distant gunfire at the range used by tourists trying out assault rifles and machine guns.

Then up popped Darren, like a meercat out of a hole, smiling broadly. "I'm used to confined spaces," he said. "I've done a bit of caving in the past." We were impressed. We noticed his knees were muddy. But then he was used to that.

Odds and Ends

This is a random mixture of tales from Austria, Ireland, Canada, Holland, Greece and Hungary.

The Shoes, Budapest, is one of the saddest tales. Budapest is a beautiful city but the horror of its 20th century history under fascist and communist regimes is somehow ever present, either in the House of Terror Museum or in the memorial of the shoes, the most poignant memorial I have ever seen.

The other tales in this section are far more light-hearted. I hope you enjoy them.

Mozart and Maria

The official in the smart suit stepped forward to bar our way. We'd held our heads high and tried to look confident as we strolled down the private drive towards the Leopoldskron Palace but the sandals, shorts and sunhats gave us away.

"Can I help you?" The young man spoke in precise English with only a hint of an Austrian accent, and in a manner which clearly suggested he didn't really want to help us at all.

"We're looking for the path round the lake," I said. I could see a wide expanse of water over his left shoulder; it was flat and shiny like glass edged with willow and pine trees. A shortcut through the grounds of the palace seemed the answer to our quest to wander round the lake where Maria and the von Trapp children had cycled and boated in a scene from the Sound of Music.

We were spending two days in Salzburg, the city where Mozart and Maria co-exist touristically speaking, and where it's easy to get confused and believe the hills are alive with the sound of Eine Kleine Nachtmusik (A Little Night Music).

We visited the Mirabell Gardens and the fountain where the children danced and sang about female deer and drops of golden sun and where today a lone duck rested on the water beneath the winged horses.

Lunch was our favourite schnitzel with noodles and later we stopped for tea, not with jam and bread but with sachertorte, the rich Austrian chocolate and apricot cake served with cream.

Then it was time for an amble by the grassy banks of the River Salbach and across the Mozart Bridge and a visit to Mozart's birthplace, on the third floor above the Spar shop, where we saw a lock of his hair, his first violin and a jewelled ring.

But now we needed to find that lake. We'd decided to walk. It looked simple on the map. We'd made our way through quiet streets and along shady, winding paths. We'd crossed a small, wooden bridge and then skirted a field of meadowsweet. A friendly Austrian woman had got off her bike to tell us the way – straight on and it's just beyond the trees. But it wasn't. Eventually we came to the driveway.

"We're looking for the path round the lake," I said again to the young man.

"Well, it's round the lake of course," the young man replied. "Not through here," he said, pointing us back the way we had come.

The hills were alive with more than the sound of music as we turned and made our way back up the drive.

We did eventually find the path and viewed the palace terrace from the other side of the lake. And to be fair to the young man, with 30,000 people visiting the city every year to relive scenes from the film, it's not surprising that he was a little exasperated by another three stragglers traipsing down the private drive.

Waking the Dead

They wake the dead every day at Newgrange. It used to be an annual event but even the long departed must bow to the demands of the modern tourist.

Newgrange, near Drogheda in Ireland, is anything but new. It is a Neolithic passage tomb, built 5000 years ago. It is older than Stonehenge and the Pyramids and so skilfully designed by the intelligent people who inhabited the Boyne Valley that at sunrise on the winter solstice, golden light fills the passage and enters the chamber where the cremated remains of their ancestors lie.

I had missed the winter solstice by two months. But even if I had arrived on time, I would not have been allowed in. More than 30,000 people buy a ticket in the annual lottery and there are only 50 lucky winners. We're not talking EuroMillions, just a chance to see the rising sun filter through, what can only be described as a giant letter box, on that special day.

I had never heard of a passage tomb until I arrived in Ireland. I was there for the Six Nations Rugby Tournament, Ireland against England, and by way of a pre-rugby distraction a friend suggested a visit to the tomb.

I had already seen some pretty ancient sights - Reginald the Viking's great tower in Waterford and abandoned villages in the wild landscape of Connemara where tumbles of rocks lay like old bones on the hillside. I'd travelled the Wild Atlantic Way and slithered up and down misty mountainsides.

As I had missed the real thing at Newgrange, I went on a guided tour there and waited for the guide to fake it. I ducked my head and squeezed between great slabs of stone, climbing along the narrow passage. "Don't enter if you suffer from claustrophobia," our guide had warned but no one bottled out.

The long passage led into a burial chamber with a 20-foot-high corbelled ceiling. This had been built with neither wheels nor metal tools and everything perfectly aligned for the sunlight to enter and presumably to waken the dead.

But no one really knows. Today it is recognised as much more than a passage tomb, more an ancient temple, a place of astrological, spiritual, religious and ceremonial importance. There has been much speculation but its true purpose remains a mystery.

I stood in the dark waiting for the guide to click the switch. As he did so a swathe of light flooded the passageway and the chamber. I was in a cathedral, a special, sacred place. I felt as though I was trespassing and disturbing an ancient peace.

The next day as wet snow plunged from a grey sky, I walked towards the 21st century rugby temple in Lansdowne Road, Dublin, where shafts of light fell from great beams in the roof. I was ready to witness a rebirth of sorts, strange rituals and much praying. I wondered whether someone might find a couple of rugby posts 5000 years hence and ponder their alignment to the sun. Would it be another of life's mysteries?

Nootka Island

The sea plane's propeller whirrs, stirring the air like an egg whisk and making the pine clad hills shimmer in the morning sunlight. I look back towards Gold River and a million stars glitter on the surface of the water. In front the flat, bottle green river flows out into the Pacific Ocean.

We arrive in a lagoon. We clamber out along the floats, drop down into knee deep water and wade ashore. We have joined two other walkers and two guides for a six-day hike on Nootka Island, a remote island off the West Coast of Vancouver Island, Canada. We're following a 30-kilometre trail from Louie Bay in the north to Yuquot in the south where a boat will take us back to the mainland. The distance seems amazingly short and I wonder how the trek will last so long.

We heave ourselves up a steep bank with a rope and struggle into the undergrowth. Our packs are heavy. We are carrying tents and food for six days. I take my first steps into the rain forest. I look ahead and see no obvious pathway. At that moment I realise why the journey will take six days. To say the terrain is difficult is an understatement. It is a mass of tangled roots and huge fallen trees. Then there are boggy areas with squelching mud.

Canopies of trailing branches hang like ships' rigging from vast cedars. The whole area is a wonderland, an endless mossy grotto plunged in shadow and a profound silence. The dense canopy is broken in places by thin shafts of sunlight. There is a quiet eerie feel and I realise that there must be bears lurking in these forests.

We arrive at Third Beach, our first stop, remove our backpacks and amble along the sand, swim in the jade waters of the Pacific, put up tents and build a fire to cook our supper. It's amazingly therapeutic, just the sound of the ocean.

We get up early and sit around the campfire, breakfasting on muffins and fried eggs, and brewing coffee. A wolf saunters out of the forest and onto the beach, glances in our direction and strolls off along the sand.

Over the next few days, the trail takes us along beaches and through forest. We watch a sea otter lazing on its back, eating fish. We watch eagles hovering overhead. We swim in icy creeks under waterfalls.

At Nameless beach we put up our tents and construct a windbreak, using the white timber that lies scattered in heaps over the beach, like the bleached bones of dinosaurs. The north-west wind is cool and the sky a dull grey. Out in the ocean a whale spouts and leaps, flicking its huge tail.

The next day we emerge from the forest onto Maquinna Point and balance precariously on the jagged black rocks, high above the bay and watch the bull kelp sway and twist with the swell of the ocean.

At dawn on day six, grey mountains glow in the early morning light. Our final push to Friendly Cove is a mere stroll with time for a lake swim before we take the boat back to Gold River.

The Wonky City

"What is the English word for this?" My walking tour guide points to a house bordering the canal in the old city of Amsterdam. It isn't straight.

"Leaning," someone calls. "Crooked" another adds.

"Ah no, the word I'm searching for is 'wonky'," Jacob replies.

Wonky seems a good word to describe the houses in Amsterdam. Leaning to the left, leaning to the right and some leaning forwards as if they might topple over. But I suppose if you build a city on mud and water, the houses will lean a little.

I had no idea the city was built on sticks. Millions of piles 15 metres long were pushed into the mud and silt after the River Amstel was dammed and the land for the city reclaimed from the North Sea. But over the years water levels have dropped in places and oxygen has crept in and some of the piles have rotted and the houses have tilted. It's all pretty random, like the rest of the city.

I am spending three wet, winter days in Amsterdam and it's full of surprises. I knew there were canals but I had no idea there were 162 plus 1500 bridges. I knew there was a bike culture but I had no idea that the 800,000 residents possessed 1.2 million bikes. Or that 10,000 of them end up in the canals every year and someone is employed specifically to fish them out.

"Beware the psychlopaths," Jacob warns. "Local cyclists are bad enough but tourists on bikes are positively dangerous." Our heads twitch nervously like frightened gazelles as we look this way and that and try to negotiate cars, trams and bikes.

But they do a different kind of cycling in Amsterdam. It's practical and purposeful. They cycle in all weather, wind and rain, and at night they fly like bats through the city, dark clothing and rarely any lights. And certainly no helmets. When they've finished cycling they park their bikes. Or they prop them, stack them, pile them up or just dump them. Every metal railing has a bike clamped to it. At the railway station a vast four storey bike park takes 3,000 and there are plans to build a bigger one to accommodate 10,000.

My initial impression was of a neat and tidy city. The train from the airport passed through new suburbs where everything was straight, the roads, apartments and office blocks. Even the trees grew tall and straight, and what little graffiti there was, looked tasteful and neat in subdued colours.

The old city is quite different. Canals, tramways and roads criss-cross, houses lean at all angles, pavements slope, clocks chime odd tunes and hymns, and cyclists roam everywhere.

After a drink or two on a canal cruise by candlelight, I begin to think that all the houses are looking a little wonky. And then I notice one standing quite straight in a row of wonky ones. It's the Irish pub.

Greek Island Heaven or Hell

I sit motionless waiting as a small puff of wind creeps over the horizon. I see a crinkle on the sea. The boat moves forward a few feet and then, like the breath of a dying man, the breeze vanishes. My skipper cannot bear to turn on the engine and fast forward us to our destination. My lot is to wait.

But then, in mid channel, half dozing with boredom I feel it, first on my cheek, then in my hair. The mast creeks and the sails begin to billow. Within minutes the wind is blustering down the channel, the boat rolling and spray flooding onto the deck. I grip with hands and feet, and pray. The Greek island of Antipaxos is still two hours away. We have not closed the hatches and the life jackets are stored away, somewhere.

We survive. The men of the flotilla shrug their shoulders nonchalantly and speak of an uncomfortable swell. The women speak of fear and drowning. One woman who has never sailed before vows to spend the rest of her days on the island. Her skipper falls off the gang plank into the sea on his way to the morning briefing.

I have a love-hate relationship with sailing. No wind and I'm bored. Too much wind and I'm scared.

My skipper has sea water coursing through his veins and does not understand.

He likes to play and is the only skipper in the flotilla to have asked for a cruising spinnaker. I watch in horror as he totters on the bow, wrestling with the wild winged creature. Eventually it fills with air and billows majestically. Twenty minutes later, he takes it down and this time he is almost overcome by the wild creature.

In a quiet cove, I lie on the deck watching the reflection of the water, dancing like flames, on the underside of the canopy. We are anchored and the boat rocks gently. This is Greek Island heaven. But is the anchor secure? Has it taken firmly into the sand or will we drift onto the rocks? And if it has taken securely, will we be able to bring it up. I am the anchorman. I glance at my anchorman's hands. I am afflicted with black nail disease. Anchor rust is embedded under my nails and cuticles. My arms ache with winch-handler's dystrophy.

There are ten boats in our flotilla and every day our leader points us in a new direction. He is competent and quite relaxed. He would not understand my fears. He warns us of 'rocky thingies' in mid channel and talks of wind force 9 and snow. I know not to take him seriously. The winds are light and it will not snow but there are 'rocky thingies' in the middle of the channel and we could hit them.

My skipper is already asking me about next year's holiday. What shall I do?

The Shoes

The sky was pigeon grey and the Danube a sludgy green on the last day, the day we walked on the stone slabs beside the river and looked at the discarded shoes, and cried.

We heard about the shoes when we arrived in Budapest. Our guide Andras, merely pointed to the river and remarked casually: "The shoes are over there but you can't see them from here."

"What shoes?" I enquired.

The moment passed and the mini bus swept over the Chain Bridge. We were climbing into the Buda hills. Andras was taking us to the Fisherman's Bastion, the Royal Palace and to the top for a magnificent view across the river to Pest. But it was raining; a fine mist lay like muslin over the city. At the top we strained our eyes and took a photo of ghostly shapes. And then Andras whipped out his mobile phone and showed us what it would have looked like on a bright sunny day.

We were spending three days in this city of beauty and terror. Three days to see the winter skaters twirling on the ice like Lowry folk; to wander along dim corridors in thermal spas and emerge, frozen feet climbing stone steps, to sit under the stars in hot mineral water.

Three days to visit markets, wood smoke curling in the air, and savour raspberry schnapps punch, and hot, sour cherry beer, and watch, just watch not taste, while a man stirred a frying pan of shiny white marble balls, which was labelled unappetizingly 'rooster testicle stew'. We had time to take a tram by the Danube and to visit the gold-filled Parliament; to cruise on the river and spend an evening at the Opera. Those were the beautiful things.

The horror came in the form of a tall grey building in Andrassy Boulevard, the House of Terror, a place of indescribable evil, where men and women were tortured and imprisoned and where their stories are told today so that all will take heed and remember Hungary's darkest moments.

In World War II Hungary became a battleground, first occupied by the Germans and then, after the siege of Budapest, by the Soviets. Hungary's own fascist Arrow Cross party committed the riverside atrocity. They ordered the Jews to line up at the water's edge and remove their shoes before they shot them into the river.

And now I knew more about the shoes, I went to look for them. As I walked beside the river. I came across a tumble of discarded shoes, old boots, tongues lolling, laces tangled, dainty shoes with heels and children's shoes, sandals with rusty buckles. No order, just abandoned.

Today the shoes are cast in iron, a memorial to the Jewish men, women and children who died. A fading red rose lay across one shoe. A candle had been placed in a child's boot. Those who live in this beautiful city still remember the horror of its past and the bravery of its people.

Acknowledgements

I want to thank my husband, Robert, for his final manuscript checking and Fiona Germaine for her final, final checking – not an easy task for either of them. I must take the blame for formatting errors. I struggled.

Printed in Great Britain
by Amazon